JEWELLERY FROM
NATURAL
MATERIALS

JEWELLERY FROM
NATURAL
MATERIALS

Beth Legg

A & C Black · London

For my Mum and Dad

FRONTISPIECE: Neckpiece, Ela Bauer, 2003. Copper-gauze & wool, 45 cm (17 ¾ in) long. Photograph by Ela Bauer.
TITLE PAGE: Peewit rings, Beth Legg. Oxidised silver.

First published in Great Britain in 2008
A & C Black Publishers Limited
38 Soho Square
London W1D 3HB
www.acblack.com

ISBN: 978-0-7136-8276-2

CIP Catalogue records for this book are available from the British Library and the US Library of Congress.

Typeset in 11 on 13pt Photina

Book design by Susan McIntyre
Cover design by Sutchinda Thompson
Commissioning Editor: Susan Kelly
Copyeditor: Julian Beecroft

Printed and bound in China

This book is produced using paper that is made from wood grown in managed, sustainable forests. It is natural, renewable and recyclable. The logging and manufacturing processes conform to the environmental regulations of the country of origin.

Contents

Acknowledgements   6

Introduction   7

1. The Origins of Natural Materials in Jewellery   9

2. A Geographical Context   13

3. A Contemporary Context   21

4. The Workshop   26

5. Stone   30

6. Shell and Coral   37

7. Bone, Antler, Horn and Tooth   42

8. Wood, Vegetable Ivory, Jet, Amber, Latex   48

9. Hair, Hides, Feathers and Wool   61

10. Cold Connections   73
   Riveting 73 • Setting 77 • Inlay 82 • Adhesive bonding 90
   Pinning 92 • Sewing 93

11. Other Applications   94

12. Contemporary Artists' Gallery   99

Galleries and Websites   136

Glossary   138

Suppliers   141

Selected Bibliography   142

Index   143

Acknowledgements

I am enormously grateful to all of the artists who have contributed their images to this book. The processes and techniques included in this book are introductory exercises intended for you to develop new techniques, skills and knowledge of materials by following advice. I hope that this will move you to apply these skills and learning to your own original ideas and pieces.

Please respect the experience, generosity and copyright of these artists by using the designs and processes included in this book in the spirit of learning.

I would like to thank Dorothy Hogg for her enthusiasm, advice and encouragement and Andy for his endless support.

Thanks also go to Chantal Knowles and Rose Watban at the National Museum of Scotland who showed and allowed me to photograph their inspirational collections.

Finally, I would like to thank A&C Black Publishers for giving me this opportunity to broaden my understanding of such a rich subject.

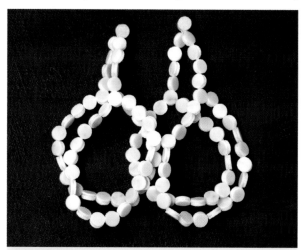

Tarja Tuupanen, 2006, brooch, marble, silver, pearlsilk, 7 x 7 x 1 cm. Photograph by Kimmo Heikkilä

6

Introduction

The roots of all things lie in nature, and the human body was almost certainly the first surface used by mankind for symbolic expression. When we look at prehistoric talismans and amulets we are confronted with the first stirrings of imaginative processes. Here humanity began forming and re-forming notions of symbolism, ritual and ceremony in an entirely intuitive manner. With this in mind the context of natural materials in jewellery is very important. I write 'context' rather than 'history' because some tribal peoples still survive against the odds and with them, exercising their ancient intuitive skills of ornamentation through the use of natural materials from their surroundings.

If nature was once the primary source of tools, materials & inspiration, and jewellery was the primary form of human expression, then the complete history of creativity lies at our feet. This book is intended to stimulate interest in further research of this vast and colourful subject. It will explore the properties of very different materials sourced from nature, and will cover some of the rich variety and methods of application available to makers when working with these fascinating materials. I freely admit that the selection of jewellers' work is entirely personal, subjective and indulgent; for me these works were equally enlightening and inspiring, and without a doubt they represent only a small part of the wealth of amazing work being produced across the globe.

When I began writing this book I had to decide how purist I was going to be in my approach to natural materials – where would I draw the 'natural' line when it comes to the materials used in jewellery today? After all, metals in their simplest forms are mineral deposits from within the Earth's crust. Is there a level of processing that negates the natural qualities of the material? Do I include mother-of-pearl and shell but not pearls, or wood and bark but not paper, or jet and jade but not diamonds? Well, the majority of pearls to be found on the market today are cultured. Paper jewellery is a rich subject and worthy of a book in itself, and highly processed gemstones, like metals, are simply outside the ambit of this book.

The jewellers whose works are included in the book show a new attitude to jewellery-making – one of uninhibited experimentation. They have in

Three brooches: *Birth*, *Tide Lines* and *Test Pieces*, Beth Legg, 2003. Burnt heather, iron, wood and silver. 7-12 cm (2¾ x 4¾ in.) long. Photograph by John K. McGregor.

common a lack of the design-orientated approach to the working process that is found elsewhere. Instead, they approach their pieces with an obvious passion for materials, thereby allowing space for the nature of those materials to speak to us in a new way.

1. The Origins of Natural Materials in Jewellery

Humans have never been content to leave their bodies in their natural state. From the very earliest times our ancestors not only drew designs on their skin with soot or ochre pigments, but devised numerous ways of attaching a variety of significant objects onto their bodies. The seemingly endless ability to invent and create symbols is one among the features that distinguish humankind from the other species that share our world, and jewellery was one of its first manifestations. In essence social beings, humans have always needed to create symbolic codes, both verbal and visual, to express themselves and communicate with others.

Relatively recent excavations at the Blombos Cave on the coast of South Africa have unearthed a set of 41 perforated snail shells which, to judge from their position, had clearly once been strung together to form

A *waseisei*, a form of necklace made of long pendants cut from sperm whale's teeth, and worn as part of a chief's regalia or offered as a gift. Fiji, Melanesia, late 19th century. Photograph by Beth Legg, courtesy of the National Museum of Scotland Collection, Edinburgh.

something like a necklace. Dating from around 100,000BC and pre-dating cave-painting, these shell pendants are considerably older than anything found in Europe and, together with the carved ochre art objects found nearby, have revolutionised thinking about the origins and history of our species. The discovery of these shell beads suggests that people had developed advanced concepts of symbol and language far earlier than was previously realised. Once symbolically mediated behaviour was adopted by our ancestors, it meant a shift in the ways we communicated with each other and the development of shared cultural values.

Around 35,000 years ago the last of the Neanderthals and the newly arrived *Homo sapiens* were living in the same parts of southern Europe. It was previously thought that the Neanderthals had simply copied the newcomers' ornaments, but careful examination of carved Neanderthal tooth pendants recently discovered in the Arcy-Sur-Cure region of France has revealed two quite distinct making techniques. While our early ancestors in Europe drilled a hole in their adornments (as in the Blombos Cave), the Neanderthals carved out a circular groove in the top of the teeth to which a string or thong might be securely attached. The indefinable and continuing similarities of jewellery techniques that are evident in distinctly different and geographically separate cultures are almost always due to the parallel restrictions of technology.

Body decoration and adornment, like verbal language, are part of the 'symbolic revolution' that constitutes the true moment when ancestors departed from the rest of the animal world. As they thrived so did ornament. No human society has ever been found that does not have body ornament in some form. These ornaments – as in the case of the snail shells and the animal teeth – might have been natural objects that were modified; or, indeed, they might not have been modified at all, for undoubtedly, although they have not survived, even earlier than 100,000BC our ancestors were almost certainly placing flowers or leaves in their hair or behind an ear. In the drive to find a greater number of ways of attaching objects to the body, cultures around the world devised techniques for piercing holes (and then sometimes enlarging these holes to impressive size) in human flesh – techniques which (long denigrated as 'primitive' in the West) are now enjoying renewed popularity in our society.

Just as no human society has ever been found which does not have some form of adornment, equally no human society has ever been found in which such adornment is without meaning. Universally, and throughout human history, the person who creates an ornament is engaging in a sociological

Ear ornament and armband from the Solomon Islands, Melanesia, late 19th century. Both made from shell, one is worn on the upper arm while the other is inserted into a stretched hole in the earlobe. Decorating the ear was one form of personal adornment common in the Solomon Islands, and these ornaments were worn by men and women from an early age. Photograph by Beth Legg, courtesy of the National Museum of Scotland Collection, Edinburgh.

activity. Even if it is primarily an aesthetically driven creation it still remains a symbol of what distinguishes man from animal. Many ornaments are never intended to be beautiful – a shaman's 'black magic' charm or a warrior's battle trophy, for instance, are specifically designed to be as horrifying as possible – but all ornaments, without exception, are intended to convey some meaning. Moreover, the vast range of properties inherent within natural materials allows for a richly poetic visual language.

For our ancestors and for those tribal peoples who, against the odds, still survive today, the meaning of ornament was inevitably social in nature. Today, in the postmodern West, the importance of ornament as signifier – as adjective – is at least as great as it was for tribal peoples, but what it has to 'say' is almost always very different. Our need is to find ornaments (a watch or a pair of glasses as much as a bracelet, brooch, necklace, piercing or pair of earrings) which visually advertise what is special about us as individuals. As well as using ornament to secure us symbolically within our tribe, we use ornament by and large to set ourselves apart as separate, distinct individuals or groups of individuals. It is not simply a matter of signifying ourselves as unique and 'interesting', but, ideally, of finding style adjectives – ornaments, decorations, accessories and garments – which, taken together as a 'style statement', summarise precisely what kind of people we think we are.

Through the symbolic value of the jewel or adornment, human beings created visual signifiers to convey cultural and social information about the bearer that helped him to define his identity: affiliation with a group, condition and status. But we often forget that as well as playing an important role in social communication, the jewel – as talisman or totem – was also a symbolic object

11

A *Kapkap*, a forehead ornament made from the concave disc of clam shell (*Tridacna*) overlaid with a circle of fretted and pierced filigree in turtle shell held on at the centre by string. Admiralty Islands, Melanesia, late 19th century. Photograph by Beth Legg, courtesy of the National Museum of Scotland Collection, Edinburgh.

that allowed man to represent himself and communicate with the invisible and transcendental world. It was this manner of defining his spiritual identity that helped him to understand and control the forces of his magic universe. Thus the amulet deflects evil while the talisman attracts good.

Unconstrained from the practical matters of keeping us warm, protected from the elements and modestly concealed, we have had to extract ever-more meaning from the medium of our appearance. Our ornaments are increasingly required to fulfil their equally practical and even-more important function of pure signification.

Scientists aim to represent the world with the least ambiguity by the use of rational thinking; artists, on the other hand, aim to represent the world by deliberately exploiting the ambiguity of intuition. If in the remote origins of jewellery the amulet and the talisman were intended to connect human beings with nature and the transcendent universe through the forces of magic, today jewellers aim to do this by integrating artistic and scientific values, resulting in jewellery that arises from new ways of thinking and working that communicate both to the maker and to the wearer. In my opinion, the creation of a contemporary jewel should be driven by the need to fulfil this function.

As long as human beings need to express themselves visually – a need that goes right back to our ancestors sitting in the Blombos Cave stringing their shell necklaces – they will always be pushing the extraordinary symbolic capacity of adornment ever further. The creation of body ornamentation always was and always will be a vital communication process.

2. A Geographical Context

The local environment has always been the primary source for materials used in adornment – immediate surroundings offering a variety of different resources in different locations around the world. Plants were probably the first jewellery-making material, providing attractive colours and forms which, though often perishable, could perform a temporary function with relatively little manipulation. From the daisy chain grew manipulations of other natural materials from the insect, animal and mineral worlds. This section provides a broad overview of the resourcefulness and creativity of some of the world's regions in using natural materials for adornment. A dialogue between man and nature is the primary focus in all of these areas.

AFRICA

African cultures demonstrate, more than any others in the world, that the urge for decoration is deep-seated in the human psyche. The people of Africa have produced jewellery of great beauty and variety since prehistoric times, and today body adornment and decoration is still abundant in every part of the African continent across all linguistic and social groups. The jewellery is deeply inspired by the rituals, beliefs and religion of the particular group that created it, while the material used naturally depends upon the geographical location, available natural resources and climate of particular region.

The use of organic materials such as bone, horn, roots, seeds, grass, etc., continues ancient tribal traditions. Masai warriors still wear a form of neckband made from a strip of goat's stomach lining ornamented with fragrant seeds embedded into the skin whilst it is still damp. A perforated disc made from a crocodile's egg shell decorates the front. Straw is also used, being one of the simplest, most compliant and most readily available materials. Grasses are woven or sewn into armbands and bracelets, while some women in northern Nigeria simply thread corn stalks through their earlobes. In the equatorial rain forest of Songhai, amber was once the material of choice, while in the old Kingdom of Benin (present-day Southern Nigeria) ivory was valued for its rich texture and supposed magical powers. In the West African forests some young women polish the pear-shaped seeds of the oil palm until they are a lustrous black. They then drill them at the tip, string them on lengths of fine rope made from the white fibres of the pineapple leaf, and wear them as pendants.

The lip plate or labret is commonly worn by women of the Surma and Mursi tribes in Ethiopia, where a lower lip plate is usually combined with the excision of the two lower front teeth, sometimes all four. In some cases a plate is also inserted into the upper lip. Other tribes, such as the Makonde of Mozambique, only wear a plate in the upper lip. Amongst Amazonian tribes, lip plates have important associations with oratory and singing, with the largest plates worn by the greatest orators and war chiefs, like the well-known environmental campaigner Raoni of the Kayapo tribe. In many older sources the plate's size is reported to be a sign of social or economical importance among some tribes. However, the plate's size often just depends on the ability of the lip to stretch at that particular stage. Lip plates are nearly always made from light wood, but they can also be found in bone or clay.

Bone, ivory and wood have been used since the earliest times. In Ghana some women still wear small bone or wooden discs inserted through a hole in their upper lip. It is the custom of women in Mozambique to have both lips pierced at the age of five, with a small piece of grass worn through the holes which are gradually enlarged as the girl grows. In the Sara and Lobi tribes, a plate is also inserted into the upper lip. By old age, these women will be wearing concave ebony discs of two or more inches in diameter. Traditions of adornment such as this are in steady decline but remain intact in some areas due to the remoteness of the regions and the continuing unadulterated adherence to tribal customs. Animal teeth, particularly the canines of large predators, were often worn threaded as pendants, as were the vertebrae of snakes and other small mammals, to form sinuous necklaces. Ivory, amber and coral were also popular.

Marine shell has long been highly valued for personal adornment in Africa. Cowrie shells can easily be adapted for use in jewellery. The dome of the shell is ground or chipped away, allowing a string to be threaded through the hole and then through the natural opening of the shell.

Amongst the earliest-known examples of African jewellery are beads made from ostrich eggshell. These were made and worn in all parts of the African Continent, and continue to be made today in Sudan and Southern Africa.

THE PACIFIC

Jewellery-making in the Pacific Islands started later than in other areas, due to their relatively recent settlement by humans. Most Pacific jewellery is worn above the waist. Headdresses, necklaces, hairpins and arm and waist belts are the most common pieces amongst island cultures. In a broadly tropical environment, body adornment did not have a sheltering or protective function and so has grown to fully exploit its ornamental value.

It is hard to date precisely when jewellery-making began on the Polynesian Islands, as many of the island nations' founders migrated there from other areas, such as Tahiti. Moreover, most early Polynesian jewellery was made of bone, wood and other natural materials, and has not survived.

One of the most recognisable pieces of jewellery tied to a Pacific culture is the Hawaiian lei. This floral necklace is given out when an outsider arrives, and has become a cultural icon for visitors to the island. On the island nation of Samoa, craftsmen from the area still use natural materials to create their jewellery, which is also often based on ancestral designs. Shells, bone, coconut and wood are all used in Samoan work.

Hei tiki, Maori, New Zealand, before 1850. Neck pendant of nephrite, carved in the form of a figure with eyes inlaid with haliotis (paua) shell, 15 cm (5 in.). Photograph by Beth Legg, courtesy of the National Museum of Scotland Collection, Edinburgh.

Elaborate headdresses are worn by many Pacific cultures; the wearing of head ornamentation being particularly common in Papua New Guinea, where there are different types of headdress to suit different occasions. These are usually made of vegetation, but designs often include bird-of-paradise feathers. Among the New Zealand Maori, the now extinct huia feather was highly prized for headdresses. Chiefs wearing white-tipped huia feathers were able to assert power over the chiefs wearing the monotone feathers of other birds. Huia feathers were revered as 'taonga', or treasures, by the Maori, and in later times also by the European settlers. The huia feathers were often grouped in pairs and were usually accompanied by a kiwi-feather cloak, an ear-piercing and commonly a small jade club. After Western colonisation, European woman began wearing the feathers to express their strong social standing.

The use of jade and hardstones has been a prominent feature of New Zealand jewellery. Carving of argillite, greywacke, basalt and, in particular, nephrite jade, also known as New Zealand greenstone, is a long-established practice in this region. Besides the terms already mentioned, nephrite has the following synonyms and varieties: aotea, axe-stone, B.C. jade, beilstein, kidney stone, lapis nephriticus, nephrit, nephrita, New Zealand greenstone, New Zealand jade, spinach jade (dark grayish green), and talcum nephriticus. Tomb jade or grave jade are names given to ancient burial nephrite pieces that have a brown or chalky white texture. Greenstone is highly valued and plays an important symbolic role in Maori culture. By the 14th century the use of greenstone was widespread among the Maori, and thus contemporary carvers and jewellers working in this material inherit a long tradition, albeit that today much of the jade is imported from British Columbia and elsewhere. Historically, Maori craftsmen carved pendants not only from the famous nephrite stone but also from whale bone and ivory, mudstone, wood and sharks' teeth. Many of these pendants were abstract representations of tools such as the fish hook, but some took the form of a bird, seal, lizard, fish or human figure. Shell and turquoise have also played an important role in ornamentation. Shell is worked by grinding, drilling, polishing and incising it with stone tools. Turquoise is most often found in the form of decorative mosaics inlaid into shell pendants. New Zealand was also the site of perhaps the most unusual example of a natural object being used as ornamentation – live birds having once been used as earrings, their beaks thrust through holes in the lobe.

Items made from string were the only garments worn by Aboriginal people in central Australia before contact with colonisers. Necklaces, breastplates, pubic tassels and ochred umbilical chords were all made from string. The material was, and continues to be, the most important item in many Aboriginal societies. Hand-spun from plant fibres, human hair and fur, and often with feathers added, string is considered to bind people both to the land and to each other. Historically, the vertebrae of sharks were used as necklaces, sometimes coloured with red ochre. Threaded seeds of many varieties are still worn as necklaces, and snail shells are often painted and used for their rattle-like qualities.

THE AMERICAS

Civilisations of intellectual accomplishment and social complexity flourished on both American Continents some 3000 years before the European discovery of the New World. Personal adornment was a highly important aspect of individual status amongst all ancient American peoples

Headdress from Guyana, South America early 20th century. Formed of rows of green, red and black feathers fastened onto a cotton band. Photograph by Beth Legg, courtesy of the National Museum of Scotland Collection, Edinburgh.

– the Peruvians and the Mesoamericans in particular. Although in many respects the cultures of the American peoples differ widely, there are basic similarities in the forms of their ornaments and in the materials used.

Organic materials have survived in the particularly arid environment of the Peruvian coast in greater amounts than in any other region of Pre-Columbian America. The surviving objects of wood, hide, fibre, feather and textile offer an insight into the multitude of adornments made and worn in ancient America that no longer exist. Impressive animal teeth and claws, radiant tropical bird feathers, delicate fish and bird bones, colourful plant fibres, lustrous human hair, iridescent beetle wings, seashells – both natural and worked – seeds, nut shells and fur are among the many natural materials utilised. The pieces including natural materials which have survived most completely tend to be constructed in mosaic and mainly consist of feather, shell, stone and bone.

Among Amazonian tribes feathers are attributed supernatural powers and their use in headdresses indicates age, status and the ethnic identity of the wearer. These associations have been lost, however, with the erosion in the autonomy of these cultures through the growth of craft production for the international market. Amazonian feather work has had a strong influence on European fashions since the 17th century. The versatility of feathers allows them to be made into a variety of adornments including necklaces, headdresses, dorsal ornaments and armbands.

Two techniques are used for feather ornamentation among Amazonian tribes. Long feathers can be attached to rigid frames to produce large and elegant constructions, or smaller feathers can be arranged on flexible frames for necklaces, crowns, etc. In some tribes, young men traditionally have their lips pierced when they enter the men's house at puberty and leave the world of women. Lip plates there carry important associations with oratory and singing, and the largest plates are worn by the greatest orators and war chiefs. They are nearly always made from light wood.

In the prehistoric period Native American Indians laboriously cut beads, earplugs and breast ornaments from local stone such as alabaster, nephrite or slate. Shell has been widely used to make necklaces, bracelets, earrings and pendants. Animal, and sometimes human, bone was used for engraved or painted gorgets (breast ornaments). Smaller, hollow bones like those of fish or birds were easily turned into tubular beads or spacers between stone beads. The Native American Indians from the south-west created hair ornaments consisting of bone points tied together to form combs and topped with tufts of feathers. Buffalo shoulder blades were cut into discs then polished and brightened with clay. Bird and animal claws were also once widely used in ear and head decoration. Grizzly-bear claws were strung on lengths of folded skin or fur as necklaces. As the grizzly population decreased, imitation claws began to be made using the horns or hooves of other animals, or even wood.

Despite the steady increase of European influences. Native American Indians continue to make use of local plants and animals. Prehistoric sites have yielded up beads made from seeds, berries and acorn cups, and today in the same area the tradition persists, with necklaces made from brightly dyed maize kernels, seeds and nuts.

The Inuit have created small adornments from ivory and bone for centuries. Living in one of the world's least forgiving climates made it necessary for them to develop carving techniques to exploit the properties of different stones in the fashioning of spear points and small implements, and also the metalworking skills that today contribute to jewellery-making. Women wore hair sticks – pieces of caribou bone around which they wound their hair – as well as copper or leather headbands decorated with animal teeth. Amulets were worn to ward

Inuit labrets, or mouth ornaments, made of limestone. Western Arctic, Canada, 1850s. Labrets were worn by men, and their shape varied according to the age of the wearer and the style of the region. Photograph by Beth Legg, courtesy of the National Museum of Scotland Collection, Edinburgh.

off evil and bring good fortune. The most common varieties of amulets were the feather of an owl, a bear's tooth, models of animals and old tools or weapons. It was often part of the shaman's responsibilities to make amulets. In Labrador, a thong of sealskin worn around the wrist was an almost universal custom. The feet of birds were also commonly worn as charms.

For decades, the worldwide artistic reputation of Canada's Inuit has been based largely on exquisite carvings of stone, antler and bone. Because of the durability of these natural materials more is known about this medium during the prehistoric period than any other form of Inuit artistic expression. Carving has grown directly out of skills developed and observations made over millennia on the land. Today's knowledge of these skills is derived from small engravings and carvings, both whimsical (doll-like figures) and spiritual (talismans), that have survived to the present day. Many of these date to the Pre-Dorset culture (2500–800BC). During the 19th and early 20th centuries, Inuit traded their representations of animals and mythical figures with whalers, explorers and other newcomers to the Arctic. Soapstone was an early favourite for its softness, but better tools have meant that harder, longer-lasting serpentine is most commonly used today. Marble, argillite and quartzite of many shades and hardnesses are also now used, as still are ivory, antler and bone.

THE VICTORIAN ERA IN EUROPE

The Victorian era was the one most noted in Europe for using natural objects in jewellery-making. Most jewellery was made from tortoiseshell, bone, ivory, coral, tiger's teeth and claws, nuts, wood, insects and hair. The Victorians also revived Egyptian design, inspired by the artefacts discovered in ancient tombs. However, the form of jewellery most associated with this period was intended for mourning.

Jet is a variety of fossilised coal. Following the death of her beloved consort Prince Albert, Queen Victoria's preference for jet made the 'black amber' hugely popular in the second half of the 19th century. The most prized and expensive form of jet is from Whitby, England, where it has been washing ashore since prehistoric times. The stone has an appearance similar to black glass, which is used as a modern substitute.

In the first stage of mourning, jet jewellery was the only ornamentation Victorian women were allowed. In the later stages jewellery made from gutta-percha, gold, pinchbeck or human hair could be incorporated into the wardrobe. Gutta-percha resembled jet but was much less expensive. A natural latex obtained from evergreen trees in East Asia, it was also the first plastic material used for costume jewellery. Today gutta-percha is used, among other things, in the manufacture of golf balls.

Mourning jewellery incorporating hair enjoyed enormous popularity in 19th-century Europe. This style which began as a simple way to keep a loved one close became an elaborate art practised by many jewellers. Taking a lock of hair and weaving it into knot designs for use in a brooch was a popular process in mourning jewellery of the period, while rings, bracelets, earrings, watch fobs and necklaces including human hair also became quite common.

Francis Willemstijn, 'Hair' necklace, 2006. Human hair, silver, glass, textile, leather, iron. 40 cm (15 3/4 in.) long. Photograph by Francis Willemstijn.

3. A Contemporary Context

Jewellery, while steeped in history and touching on notions of wealth, position and desire, has shifted to realise its potential to engage with postmodern ideals. Contemporary makers follow their own individual artistic drives and no longer feel duty-bound to the dictates of traditional jewellery-making in either form or material.

Some jewellery makers have shaken off the burden of tradition and issues of preciousness by adopting an anti-gold ethos – a democratisation of jewellery. The return to natural materials, which are currently being used globally and in all manner of combinations, demonstrates a more intuitive attitude in the working process of the jewellery maker. In recent years a plethora of resources has been applied to jewellery-making, evidence of artists seeking refuge in materials that do not require a maker's mark.

The issue of the value of a material may be losing its validity, but good workmanship is as important in working with natural materials as it is with silver and gold. Makers have a wide range of decisions to make about how a material is applied and how it looks, to what level they work it and how much their touch might bring to it. Natural materials are often reworked to emphasise

Timber brooch, Terhi Tolvanen, 2007. Rosemary wood, silver, graphite, paint, 18 cm (6 in.). Photograph by Francis Willemstijn.

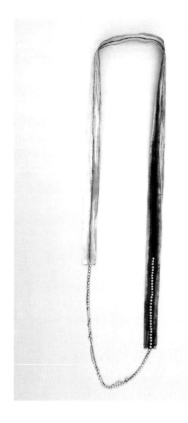

Tracing Memory 2, Hsiu-Hsuan Huan, 2006. Silk sheet, ink, pearl, silk, 56 cm x 15 cm (22½ x 5 in.). Photograph by Hsiu-Hsuan Huan.

their fundamental aesthetic values. In contemporary jewellery-making the raw material is often a concept or idea, and the preciousness of the jewellery piece lies in the extent of the process applied to it.

The pre-modern view of nature as a well-oiled machine of God's creation has been replaced by the realisation, in the teeth of growing evidence, that nature is not perpetually self-renewing but finite. Contemporary art that concerns itself with nature has become burdened with guilt.

Material and object, whether natural or man-made, can raise these issues. The jewellery industry and individual jewellers use many products that damage and corrode the earth, and are toxic to jewellers themselves as well as the environment. Materials which have proved hazardous to the wearer have been banned. Ethically unacceptable materials such as elephant ivory or tropical butterfly's wings, the use of which has had a negative impact on populations of threatened species, no longer find support amongst consumers. Efforts have increased to minimise, even eliminate, damage to natural resources through the introduction of modifications to practice and the use of alternative materials within the jewellery industry.

Improved opportunities for travel have exposed today's artists to different materials and increased cross-cultural influence. The cultural values attached to certain materials persist, however, with jewellery makers valuing some materials for belonging to their own traditions. For example, wood might be seen as especially important to Scandinavians and mother-of-pearl to Australians.

The use of found materials involves both a social attitude and an artistic pleasure: form, shape, texture and colour are often ready-made. The found object's potential is exploited both for its vernacular qualities and as pure form and volume. The symbolism and associations attached to these objects are very personal to both artist and audience. Real fragments from the environment are often used to challenge the viewer – a metaphoric, as opposed to imitative, reference to the world.

An issue of interest to many contemporary jewellers is that no material is neutral. In fact, many materials are intentionally used for their metaphoric possibilities. Most viewers will see the parallels between the history of an object and the history of a person's life, though not necessarily on a conscious level. Moreover, in using materials with such a range of associations, a jewellery maker can imply a level of symbolism inseparable from a material's actual qualities.

The function of natural material as a component part of any piece of jewellery will inevitably differ from that of orthodox material. As element is set beside element, the many qualities of isolated fragments are either enhanced or contradicted or subsumed into the visual poetry of a piece.

Brooch, Bettina Speckner, 2004. Volcanic stone, tourmaline, coral, enamel, silver, 4 cm x 5.5 cm (1½ x 2¼ in.). Photograph by Bettina Speckner.

Lola necklace, Lucy Sarneel, 2005. Wood from an old washing-up brush, zinc, silk string. Neck-opening diameter 14 cm (5½ in.). Photograph by Ron Zijlstra.

The range of expression possible is different in kind from painting and sculpture but akin to literature. Combining objects that attract or repel, natural or human identification, ironic or naïve responses, allows an artist to work simultaneously on several different, often provocative, levels.

Many makers assume a critical approach to the tradition of creating and wearing jewellery, questioning local customs – clichés and stereotypes – associated with certain materials. The individual approach of each maker in this case becomes crucial, the key aim being not to enclose themselves within the narrow frame of the genre, with each piece attempting to link past and present ways of working.

Often, makers who intuitively create works inspired by the natural object cannot offer a logical reason for their choices. In many cases form and expression arise simultaneously, and grow and develop through observation and practice, trial and error. Many material combinations are chosen not so much for their physical qualities, but using abstract associations such as lightness, transparency or elasticity. This process is metaphysical and poetic as well as physical and realistic. The eye, an imaginative mind and the skill of the hand combined can invest a dormant object with a new life, form and context.

Including a natural object within a piece jewellery evokes the naive delight of childhood at finding objects on the beach or in the forest. Today people are often distanced from their natural surroundings, and jewellery from natural materials can perhaps play a small part in reconnecting them.

By combining a variety of different materials – for instance, metal, wood, leather, stone, hair – the maker is demonstrating a belief that no material in itself is more valuable than another. A piece of wood, just like gold, may be both banal and expressive. The potential for plastic expression within the material is considered to be crucial.

Brooch, Beth Legg, 2007.Carved alabaster & oxidised silver. Approx. 12 cm long. Photograph by Beth Legg.

The use of an organic object is a method by which the artist can directly link man and environment. Using objects taken directly from the environment asserts the relationship between humanity and the natural world, one of the richest themes in contemporary art.

At its best, contemporary jewellery in this field demonstrates great intuitive compositional skill. The work seems not to imitate but to be analogous to the processes and conditions of nature itself.

4. The Workshop

It's essential when starting out to get the right tools for the job. A basic jeweller's kit is perfectly adequate for working with most natural materials included in this book.

- Emery sticks
- Flat and half-round files
- A range of needle files
- Saw frame and blades
- Archimedean drill
- Steel centre punch
- Steel rule

- Steel scribe
- Pliers – round-nose, flat and half-round
- Steel block
- Wire-cutters
- Snips
- A selection of hammers and mallets

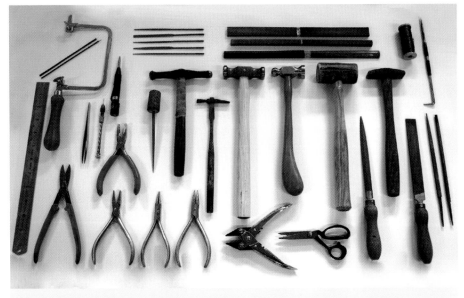

The basic toolkit

For larger jobs you might need more heavy-duty equipment such as a strong vice and a hacksaw.

Other useful equipment includes masking tape, scalpel blades, scissors, pencil, Blu-Tack, permanent marker, threads and needles, and wet-and-dry sandpapers.

HEALTH AND SAFETY

You are the best person to take charge of your own safety. When you enter a workshop environment please think carefully about how you dress. The general rules are to wear sturdy shoes, tie back long hair, remove jewellery and wear older clothes that cover you or an apron. Always segregate your working and eating/drinking areas, and remember to keep a well-equipped first-aid kit in your studio. Hand-tool operations are less likely to seriously injure you; it is certainly possible, but it's a lot harder to hurt yourself badly with a hand tool than with a power tool. Most operations in jewellery-making are hand-tool based so the accident rates are comparatively low when measured against those of other industries. When dealing with power tools always have a great deal of respect for them.

DUSTS

Ventilation is very important. Dusts you can see in the air can be breathed in – the particles are fairly large and thus end up in the upper parts of the lungs. However, the smaller, invisible dust particles are more dangerous, as these travel far deeper into the lungs and can result in chronic damage.

Many kinds of dust, and even metal particles in fumes, are this tiny. Because they are so small, they float in the air for hours, and merely moving about lifts the settled ones back into the air for you to breathe in later. When they are this small they are easily bound up and stay put in your lungs, or may even be absorbed through the lungs directly into your bloodstream. Wherever you can see dust in the air you can be sure that these smaller dangerous particles are also present.

Be aware of the things you do that generate dusts; for jewellers this usually means using abrasive procedures, i.e. sanding, grinding and polishing. Consider the kind of material you are working with and what are the implications of turning it into a dust. Some woods, shells and other materials can be extremely toxic when made into dusts and inhaled or touched. Asthma-causing materials include pine resin, iroko, mahogany, western red-cedar woods, and animal and insect proteins. Where you can, choose the least dust-producing materials, techniques and processes possible and, if viable, use localised ventilation that takes the dust away from where you are producing it, removing it safely from your workplace.

Dust produced when cutting, grinding, polishing or drilling shells and stones can be hard on your lungs. A particulate respirator should be worn when undertaking heavy-duty production work or if you're particularly sensitive to dust. It's also a good idea to protect your eyes with safety goggles. Always keep the grinding wheels and stone or shell wet to reduce airborne dust, to keep the work cool, and to prevent the wheels from clogging. Water is the most common coolant used. If you generate dusts or fumes and are exposed to chemicals as a result of your working methods, take full responsibility for what you are doing. If possible, work wet so that particles cannot become airborne – for instance, sand using wet-and-dry paper in trays under a little water. Damp-mop and wipe your studio and work area rather than vacuuming or sweeping. In general, don't have dusts around if you can help it, but if you have to create them, store the materials properly, damp-clean frequently, segregate dust-producing procedures from the rest of your studio, and where possible work wet. NB: Remember to exercise caution when using electrical equipment around water. All machinery should have an R.C.D. or safety switch fitted.

BURNS

Burns are a common hazard in the jewellery workshop. Don't use oils or greasy ointments to treat a burn first. The best treatment is to freeze a burn as soon as possible. Burn damage keeps on going for some time after the cause

The basic equipment to keep you protected – rubber gloves, dust mask and goggles.

of the burn is removed, so if you freeze it fast enough and keep it cold for a while you can often limit the damage considerably. The juice from the leaves of an aloe vera plant can hasten healing and sooth burns, but it is still best to apply ice or run under a cold tap for a long time in the first instance.

REPETITION

Do not perform repetitive tasks for too long without a break, as any action repeated over and over again has the potential to injure the joint where it is repeatedly flexed and stressed. Vibration injuries, sometimes called 'white finger', can occur to machine operators and polishers. Try and arrange your jobs so you work in different ways and use your body differently during the day. A ten-minute break, as well as changing to a different activity, every 45 minutes helps avoid this kind of joint damage. Much damage could be avoided by having different working heights – makers often perform the wrong task at the bench-pin height because that is the main height available to them. Some tasks should be done at waist height and others elsewhere. Particularly if you're doing the same job over and over again all day, as occurs when producing a run of similar pieces, it can help dramatically to be able to work at varying heights during the day.

SIGHT

Make sure that you have adequate lighting if you are performing detailed work. To avoid eye strain and headaches, every 20 minutes refocus your sight on a spot in the distance – at least 20 feet away – in order to relax your eye muscles.

5. Stone

Human beings have been creating art from stone ever since they found that a softer stone could be shaped by striking it with a harder one. The earliest examples of stone-carving are the result of just this method, although sometimes more resilient materials such as antlers are known to have been used for relatively soft stone. Another early technique was to use an abrasive that was rubbed on the stone to remove the unwanted area.

Marble, alabaster and soapstone are known as metamorphic rocks. These are formed when a sedimentary layer is exposed to heat and pressure and undergoes a chemical change to form a new crystalline material. For instance, after metamorphism limestone becomes marble.

Marble has been the stone most preferred for carving since the time of the ancient Greeks. Marble is moderately hard to work but will hold very fine detail. Marbles from the United States come in over 250 colours. When brought to a high polish, its crystalline structure sparkles. It does not hold up well outdoors, as acid rain begins to deteriorate the surface within a few years.

Alabaster is a very soft stone to use for carving and tends to flake and split along hidden cracks in the stone. However, it will take a high polish, which brings out its incredible colours and patterns. In fact alabaster is so beautiful that the viewer may overlook your sculptural forms in simply admiring the stone. The dust from alabaster may cause an allergic reaction in some people, so wear a respirator if you are working with it.

Soapstone, or steatite, is soft enough to carve with a knife. Composed of talc, it has a slippery, soapy feel. It will take a polish and hold fine-textured detail. It is a good choice for your first stone carving. Prolonged exposure to talc dust can cause respiratory problems, so, once again, wear a respirator if you're planning to use it.

Jade has extreme toughness and specific aesthetic qualities which become more pronounced with handling. Working with jade is not for the novice and requires specialist diamond-cutting tools as it is very resilient. Carving hardstone remains a time-consuming activity. Despite advances in technology which have speeded up the process, sawing, grinding, drilling and polishing remain the fundamental and unvarying techniques.

Brooch, Tarja Tuupanen, 2006. Onyx, rubber, silver, 6 x 2 x 2 cm (2⅜ x ¾ x ¾ in.). Photograph by Jaan Seitsara.

Extraordinary concentrations of time and human skill are invested in even the smallest carved jade object and so, with every finished piece comes a distillation of unseen qualities such as perseverance and respect.

SAFE STONEWORK

The first rule of safety when carving stone with hand or pneumatic tools is to wear safety glasses. Depending on the type of stone, the chips thrown up during carving can be as sharp as glass shards. Your eyes are your most valuable tool; protect them.

Unfinished alabaster chunks – this stone has a lovely milky quality. I love its opacity, but it is tricky to work as it often has many hidden fissures.

Alabaster can be worked with hand tools alone and is easily sawn or filed into shape.

A quality dust mask is also required when carving or sawing some stones, especially those containing silica, such as granite or soapstone. As always, wear a respirator when creating dust.

Anti-vibration gloves protect hands from the constant vibration of pneumatic tools and a wrist support will help prevent carpal-tunnel injury.

Keep a well-equipped first-aid kit handy.

STONE-CARVING

There are two basic approaches to carving. The first is to work with what nature has given you. Find a stone with a distinctive shape or colour pattern that might suggest a structure or form. This approach will free you to follow the natural directions within the material. The qualities of the stone itself become a major influence in determining the direction of the form.

The second approach is to begin by working out an idea for the form in drawings, or by first modelling a maquette in clay or plasticine. This is most useful if you are carving a more complex three-dimensional shape. Ideas about a piece have a tendency to change as you work on it, so modelling in clay first – when you can add and subtract material, push and twist the forms around, and try different combinations – frees you to develop the sculptural idea without worrying about taking off a chunk of stone that you might later wish to have back.

Before you begin carving, look at the stone to determine the direction of the bed or grain, in the way you'd work with wood. In sedimentary, metamorphic

Closing Time brooch, Joe Sheehan, 2005. New Zealand jade, paint and silver, 6 x 6 cm (2³/₈ x 2³/₈ in.). Photograph by Nick Barr.

and to a lesser extent igneous rock, the stone was formed by the accumulation of roughly parallel layers of material built up over time. Wetting a stone with water will help display these bed lines, which often appear as distinctive colour patterns.

Stone will tend to break more easily when split along these bed lines, like opening the pages of a book. And, like trying to tear a phonebook, it is more difficult to break and breaks less predictably when the direction is perpendicular to the bed lines.

As with wood-carving, when laying out a design in stone you must also consider the direction of the grain to safeguard its structural integrity. Try to keep the grain running with the length of the design, and avoid thin projections that protrude parallel to the grain. Once you have determined the direction of the bed, check to see if there are any hairline cracks in the stone that could open up and break off later during carving. When drawing your design, mark with

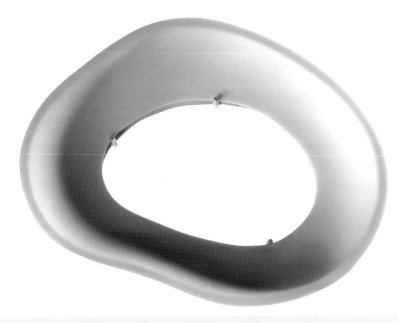

Brooch, Tarja Tuupanen, 2006. White quartz, silver, 6.5 x 4 x 1 cm (2½ x 1½ x ½ in.). Photograph by Jaan Seitsara.

pencil on all sides of the stone. Continuously rotate the piece of stone in order to ensure you are projecting the same height and width on all sides.

STONE-POLISHING

Polishing brings out the natural colour and pattern of a stone. With the softer stones, continue hand-sanding with the wet-and-dry sandpaper under running water. Work through the grits by roughly doubling the number of the last grit, proceeding in stages from a rough 150 grit up to somewhere between 600 and 3000, in order to obtain your desired level of polish. On the harder stones, you might want to use a motorised polisher or diamond pads in an assortment of grits ranging from 40 to 3000.

After you have finished thoroughly going over the piece with a particular grit, let the stone dry. Check to see if there are any scratches or other imperfections that were not removed by the last grit. Mark the blemishes with a coloured pencil and go over the area again with the last grit until all the blemishes are removed before proceeding to the next, finer grit.

Note that if you have gone through all the grits but did not stop and dry the stone to check for scratches, you may be shocked at the end to find

Brooch, Laura Saarnia, 2007. Quartz, silver, Lazertran, 6 x 4 cm (2³⁄₈ x 1¹⁄₂ in.). Photograph by Kimmo Heikkilä.

scratches left in the otherwise beautiful finish. If this happens you will have to start all over again from the beginning.

DRILLING HOLES IN STONE

Drilling a hole in stone will allow you to apply cold connections such as riveting or pinning. It can also be used purely as an aesthetic choice.

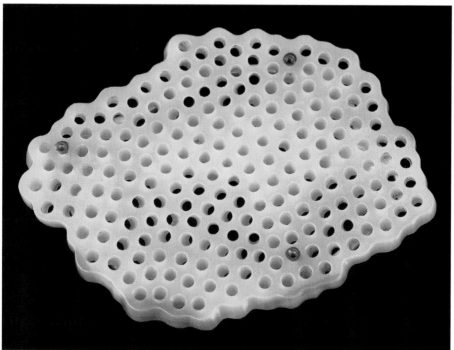

Cloud brooch, Joe Sheehan, 2005. Russian jade and silver, 6 x 4 cm (2³⁄₈ x 1¹⁄₂ in). Photograph by Nick Barr.

Equipment

- A diamond drill bit of your chosen size
- An electric drill (preferably pendant but flexi-shaft can work also)
- A drill vice
- Water (in a tub or spray)

Note that drilling is best done with a pillar or bench drill. If you tweak the bit, it will snap apart, so it's important to hold the bit perfectly perpendicular to the stone.

Diamond bits are meant to be kept wet whilst in use. The bit doesn't need to be in a lot of water, just enough to wash away the rock mud and keep it moist. The easiest way to accomplish this is to do your drilling in a bin or tub of water. A ceramic dish works well; a spray or sponge will also be fine. Another way of keeping the stone wet is to have a drip system continually dripping water onto the point you are drilling. Once you start drilling, use a very gentle up/down motion to allow fresh water under the bit. If you slam your bit down on the rock, you will knock off the diamonds, making your bit ineffective.

By following these steps your bits should perform at their maximum drilling capacity.

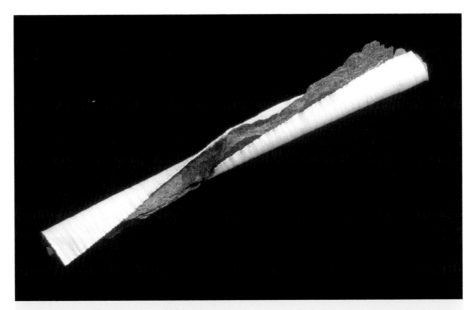

Slate brooch, Beth Legg, 2003. Scottish slate and silver, 12 x 1.5 cm (4³/₄ x ⁵/₈ in.). Photograph by Beth Legg.

6. Shell and Coral

SHELL

A shell is the rigid outer covering, or exoskeleton, of certain animals. A shell can be made of nacre (a combination of calcium and protein), bone or cartilage. While many sea animals produce exoskeletons, usually only those of molluscs are considered to be 'seashells'.

The shell will grow over time as the animal inside adds its building material to the leading edge near the opening. This causes the shell to become longer and wider to better accommodate the growing animal inside. A mollusc shell is formed, repaired and maintained by a part of the mollusc called the mantle. Injuries to, or abnormal conditions in, the mantle are often reflected in the shell it forms and tends. When the animal encounters harsh conditions which limit its food supply or otherwise cause it to become dormant for a while, the mantle often ceases to produce the shell substance.

Brooch (front & back), Bettina Speckner, 2004. Ferrotype, silver, Labradorite fossil, snail shells, 9.5 cm (3³/₄ in.). Photograph by Bettina Speckner.

When conditions improve again and the mantle resumes its task, a 'growth line' is produced that extends the entire length of the shell; the pattern and even the colours on the shell after these dormant periods are sometimes quite different from previous colours and patterns. Interestingly, each species of mollusc animal will build the external shell in its own specific shape, pattern, ornamentation and colour.

Untitled, Sebastian Buescher, 2007. Earthenware, Russian jade, resin, limpet, gold, amber, silver, 8 x 2 cm (3 $^1/_8$ x $^3/_4$ in.). Photograph by Sebastian Buescher.

Brooch, Lucy Sarneel, 2003. Shells filled with epoxy, silver, antique textile. Approx. 10 x 7 x 4 cm (4 x 2¾ x 1½ in.). Photograph by Ron Zijlstra.

Shells are composed of calcium carbonate. When a mollusc is invaded by a parasite or is irritated by a foreign object that the animal cannot eject, the mollusc entombs the offending entity in successive, concentric layers of nacre. This process eventually forms what we call pearls, and continues for as long as the mollusc lives. Almost any species of bivalve or gastropod is capable of producing pearls, but only a few kinds, such as those produced by the famous pearl oysters, are highly prized.

CORAL

Coral is not a mineral but a hornlike skeleton of calcium carbonate and organic matter. Corals are marine animals existing as small sea anemone-like polyps, typically in colonies of many individuals. The Romans believed coral could protect children from harm, cure wounds made by snakes and scorpions, and diagnose diseases by changing colour.

Corals are major contributors to the physical structure of the coral reefs that develop in tropical and subtropical waters. Its unique and striking colour has made red coral a popular gemstone choice for jewellers in recent years. Pure red coral, also known as 'fire coral' or 'ox-blood coral', is becoming very rare due to high demand for the

Ring, Ela Bauer, 2005. Copper gauze, silicone, coral, 2 cm (³/₄ in.). Photograph by Ela Bauer.

perfect specimens used in the jewellery industry. Red coral is a semi-translucent-to-opaque material that is frequently dyed to enhance its natural colour. The black and red corals used in jewellery are calcareous corals, much softer than other gems, with a hardness of only 3.5 to 4.0 on the Mohs scale. Fire-red coral has a waxy-to-vitreous lustre. Corals can also be impregnated with resins or epoxies to fill surface fissures and flaws.

Reconstituted coral is made from natural solid material or coral fragments which have been pulverised into a powder, soaked in binding agents and then pressed into a solid mass to be recut. It can also be dyed to enhance colour.

Necklace, Julie Mollenhauer, 1997. Blue coral, silver. 18 x 18 x 0.5 cm
(7 x 7 x ⅕ in.). Photograph by Thomas Lenden.

Over-collection is putting stress on the environmental health of coral reefs, and thus the ethical sourcing of coral is vitally important; where you can, use reclaimed or antique pieces.

Working with shell and coral

The dust created by the grinding and cutting of shell is dangerous, so appropriate safeguards should be taken to prevent you inhaling its particles. Wet grinding, a ventilation system and the use of a dust respirator that is safety-approved for fine particles are essential requirements for working safely with shell. The calcium carbonate found in shells, especially the popular abalone, is a respiratory hazard: if they get into the lower respiratory tree, the particles can cause bronchitis and other respiratory illnesses.

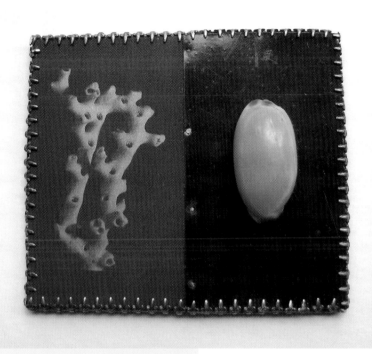

Brooch, Bettina Speckner, 2004. Zinc photo-etching, silver, cowrie shell, ferrotype, 6.8 x 5.8 cm ($2^5/_8$ x $2^1/_4$ in.). Photograph by Bettina Speckner.

RIGHT Untitled, Sebastian Buescher, 2007. Earthenware, silver, metal, resin, gold, coral, 8 x 3 cm ($3^1/_8$ x $2^1/_4$ in.). Photograph by Sebastian Buescher.

Dust suppression by using water in all stages of the cutting and polishing process will minimise both of those problems, and latex gloves will keep the worker 'mud-free'. The water also keeps the material being cut from overheating and developing opaque white spots during the grinding and polishing phases.

7. Bone, Antler, Horn and Tooth

The use of these biological materials as tools and forms of adornment has been prevalent since ancient times. In particular, they have been commonly used for piercings by many cultures. Today, with advances in tissue engineering we can grow bone cultured from human cells, and jewellery made from lab-grown bone tissue is now a reality.

Bone, antler, horn and tooth are the ethical alternative to ivory, but the issues that surround the use of them, as with all naturally sourced materials, still have to be kept in mind. Know where your supplies come from and, where possible, utilise waste products.

WORKING WITH BONE, ANTLER, HORN AND TOOTH

Bone, antler, horn and tooth all have a similar morphology, so in this chapter I will refer to all four as 'bone'. Working these materials is not unlike working hardwoods, as they are easily shaped and can be worked into a smooth surface. When you wear them, these organic materials allow your body to 'breathe' and they never get cold. However, like wood they can dry out, which sometimes leads to cracking.

Iris Eichenberg, 2004. From the 'Heimat' series. Gold, silver, bone. 14 x 6 cm (5$\frac{1}{2}$ x 2$\frac{2}{3}$ in.). Photograph by Ron Zijlstra.

Another thing that can cause bone to crack is heat. This is the most important point to remember when working these materials, as nearly all cracks that occur in worked bone that has been properly cured are caused by overheating due to improper techniques when using machines for cutting, sanding and polishing the material.

Note that when working the bone dry, wear a dust mask. Bone dust is not toxic, but considering the fine dust particles produced, wearing a dust mask makes sense. Also remember that bone is a porous substance and is prone to some shrinkage as it dries; consider this when setting or pinning it into metal. Sealing it with oils after shaping should slow or stop the shrinkage.

When working with bone, it is helpful to be aware of certain processes that make it easier to transform a fresh bone just removed from a pork roast into a completed object such as a ring. Most contemporary bone-carving is made using beef bone, which is generally quite white and clean-grained – much like a cheap and ethical version of ivory. The finish that can be achieved is high and holds good detail. Beef bone is readily available and has little grain to combat.

SOURCES AND TYPES

I source the bones I work with from the beach – these bones have been bleached and cleaned naturally by the sun and the tides – but you can easily obtain bones from other places depending on what you are looking for. Usable-sized pieces of pork, beef, lamb and turkey bone are all readily available from store-bought fresh meat, as well as from processed meat such as smoked ham. To obtain whole bones or a quantity of bones, however, you would need to contact a local meat-processing plant. Pet stores are a good source for clean beef leg bones. Use long leg bones for thin and delicate lengths, thick-walled bones for chunky sections, shoulder blades for a larger surface area and bird leg bones (turkey, goose, etc.) for small, light, hollow pieces.

BONE PREPARATION

1. Remove as much meat as possible from the fresh bone.
2. Boil the bone until the remaining meat, tendons, etc., are falling off, making sure that the water covers the bone at all times. (Do not bake the bone, as baking makes the bone more brittle.)
3. Allow the bone to cool to the point where it can be handled.
4. Trim off all remaining bits of cartilage, gristle and exposed marrow with a knife.

5. For hollow bird bones you might need to clean out marrow with a file.
6. Scrub the bone under hot running water with a scrubbing pad.
7. Allow the cleaned bone to air-dry.

CUTTING & ROUGH-SHAPING

Use dry bone when sawing. Wet bone is more difficult as it quickly gums up the saw teeth. Bone can be cut with any tool that will cut wood: a hacksaw with coarse teeth, a jeweller's saw or a band saw. The fewer teeth per inch the less clogging with dust; but the more teeth per inch the smoother the cut and the less subsequent sanding required. Use a reasonably fine-toothed saw blade to trim the bone as close as possible to its final shape. With any saw, a sharp blade is essential, as a dull blade will result in rough wandering cuts at best and scorched bone at worst. This is the same when using drill bits, burrs and sandpaper: the easier it cuts the cooler it cuts.

FINE-SHAPING

Use wet bone to cut with a knife. If the bone has totally dried out, soak it for a day or so in water. If the bone dries out as you are working it, let it soak

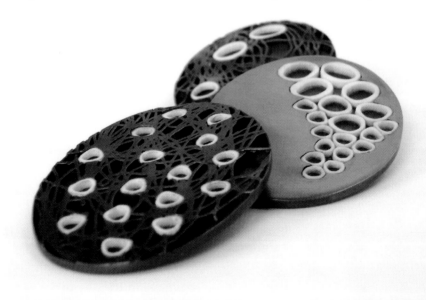

Three *Caged Bird* brooches, Beth Legg, 2006. Bird bone, oxidised silver, 4.5 x 7 cm (1³/₄ x 2³/₄ in.). Photograph by Beth Legg.

again for a while until it is easy to cut again. Use a very sharp knife, such as a scalpel blade, to shape the bone to its final form.

Remember always to wear some sort of thumb guard to protect the thumb you are carving towards. Leather quilting thimbles work well, but a simple leather guard can easily be sewn. Make sure it covers most of the thumb.

Use dry bone for file work.

FINISHING

Bone can be worked very finely with a knife. As it is worked, it will also become smoother due to the oils from the carver's fingers. When sanding bone make sure you use fresh sandpaper or sanding belts that are good and 'sharp'. Wet sanding with wet-and-dry paper is best for sanding bone, as there is no dust and no heat. To wet-sand use a bucket of water or the sink and wet the paper and/or the bone enough to keep the bone dust/paste off both the paper and the bone piece; this way, the paper never gets clogged, there is no dust, the paper lasts much longer and there is no heat. Whether you dry-sand or wet-sand you should start out with a coarse grit paper to remove the saw marks. Don't rush from one grade of paper to the next before you have removed the scratches from the previous grit: you will either end up going back to the previous grit to remove earlier deep scratches, or you will spend more time trying to get them out with the fine grit paper.

Use an emery board or sandpaper to finish off any remaining rough edges. Getting a mirror-smooth finish by hand can take practice; try rubbing with a metal polish or auto-polishing compound on a rag. The best results come from a fast-spinning buffing or polishing wheel. If using a polishing wheel, don't hold the piece in one spot or press it hard into the wheel. Use white rouge to put the glassy sheen on the

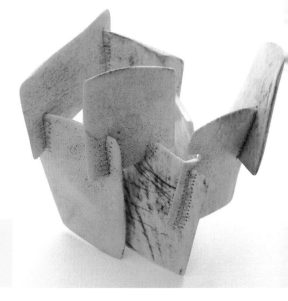

Arm piece, Caroline Holt, 2007. Bone & 18 ct gold, 10 x 11 cm (4 x 4¼ in.). Photograph by Caroline Holt.

Dust to Dust ring, Kelly McCallum, 2006. Human bone, plant. Approx 5 x 2 x 1.5 cm (2 x ³/₄ x ¹/₂ in.). Photograph by Kelly McCallum.

bone. Red rouge works but is messy and gets hot. Overheating cooks the splendour out of fresh bone. This telltale symptom of overheating is a sure sign that crazing (tiny cracks) will follow.

Mineral oil will help protect the bone from shrinking or cracking due to a dry climate and lack of humidity; this works best with slabs and thin pieces. Place the unpolished slabs in mineral oil for several days, then remove, wipe off and store in a plastic bag until you're ready to use them; the bone will absorb some oil and after being sanded and polished will allow even less moisture to escape, thereby reducing the possibility of shrinking and cracking. Your natural skin oil, rubbed on bone as you work it, will also help start to colour it slightly.

Note that if you are riveting into bone, drill the holes just a little oversized and fill the gap with glue. This allows for shrinkage – bone expands and contracts, and tight pins can cause cracking.

When storing horn or bone in any form – raw, sliced or finished – the best policy is to keep it in an area that has a high humidity.

CARVING SURFACE DESIGNS

Incise the lines of the surface design using a sharp knife on wet bone. If it is difficult to see the lines, use a pencil or let the bone dry out a little.

Widen the lines by scraping along them using the edge of a knife, scribe or some other similar object on the dry bone. This makes it possible to carefully control the degree of bone removal.

If desired, use one of the historical methods of enhancing the carving such as painting the lines, or differentiate the background from the pattern with cross-hatching or other fillers.

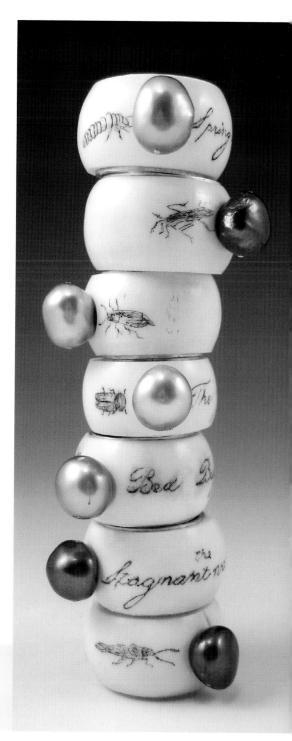

Seven *Insect Rings*, Kristin Beeler, 2007. Bone, pearl, ink, 2.5 x 3 cm (1 x 1¼ in.). Photograph by Kristin Beeler.

47

8. *Wood, Vegetable Ivory, Jet, Amber, Latex*

WOOD

When working with wood we are constantly reminded that it was once a living organism. Its natural qualities – knots, textures, grain and tones – all speak of the growth and life of the tree and can be most attractive qualities to work with. Wood is light and is easy to carve, file and polish, and thus lends itself well to application in jewellery.

Ronde Stipjes necklace, Tehri Tolvanen, 2006. Silver, wood, paint, 16 cm (6¼ in.) diameter. Photograph by Eddo Hartmann.

Cross brooch, Francis Willemstijn, 2006. Silver, bog oak. 9 x 7 x 3 cm (3½ x 2¾ x 1⅛ in.). Photograph by Francis Willemstijn.

Clearly there is a strong relationship between the properties of wood and the properties of the particular tree that yielded it. Wood is commonly classified as either softwood or hardwood, the wood from conifers (e.g. pine) being called softwood, and the wood from broad-leaved trees (e.g. oak) referred to as hardwood. However, these names are a bit misleading, as hardwoods are not necessarily hard, and softwoods are not necessarily soft. The well-known balsa, a hardwood, is actually softer than any commercial softwood. Conversely, some softwoods (e.g. yew) are harder than most hardwoods.

The abnormal discoloration of wood often denotes a diseased condition or can indicate unsoundness. The black check in western hemlock is the result of insect attacks, while the reddish-brown streaks so common in hickory and certain other woods are mostly the result of injury from birds. However, these discolorations are merely indications of a small injury. In all probability they do not affect the properties of the wood,

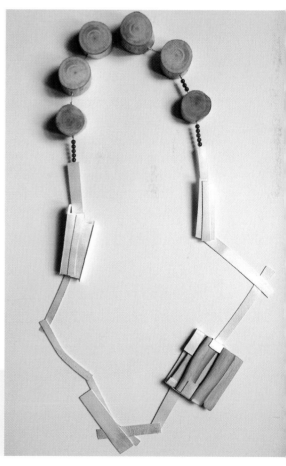

Roadmap necklace, Helga Ragnhildur Mogensen, 2006. Driftwood, silver, cornelian. 89 cm (35 in.). Photograph by Helga Ragnhildur Mogensen.

and in fact they often add to the personality of it. Certain rot-producing fungi sometimes pass on their characteristic colours to wood. This can also be symptomatic of weakness, though an attractive effect known as spalting produced by this process is often considered a desirable characteristic. Ordinary sap-staining is due to fungus growth but does not necessarily produce a weakening effect.

If ease of working rather than natural character is what you would like, then a piece of wood should be chosen with regard to its uniformity of texture and straightness of grain. In most cases this will occur when there is little contrast between the late wood of one season's growth and the early wood of the next.

Heartwood and sapwood

Sapwood is living wood in the growing tree. All wood in a tree is first formed as sapwood. Its principal functions are to conduct water from the roots to the leaves and to store up and give back according to the season the food prepared in the leaves. The more leaves a tree bears and the more vigorous its growth, the larger the volume of sapwood required. Hence trees making rapid growth in the open have thicker sapwood for their size than trees of the same species growing in dense forests.

As a tree increases in age and diameter an inner portion of the sapwood becomes inactive and finally ceases to function as the cells die. This inert or dead portion is called heartwood. Its name derives solely from its position and not from any vital importance to the tree. This is shown by the fact that a tree can thrive with its heart completely decayed. Some species begin to form heartwood very early in life, and thus have only a thin layer of live sapwood, while in others the change comes slowly. Thin sapwood is characteristic of such trees as chestnut, black locust, mulberry and sassafras, while thick sapwood is the rule in maple, ash, hickory, hackberry, beech and pine.

Heartwood is preferred for woodworking, as it is far less susceptible to fungus and doesn't contain nearly as much moisture as sapwood,

Sycamore wood sliced lengthways to illustrate the heartwood and sapwood sections. Photograph by Beth Legg.

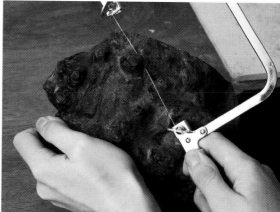

Knots can be sawn off relatively easily but often have hidden weaknesses as well as interesting grains.

meaning it will shrink less when dried. While the sapwood will never be as strong, rich or beautiful as the heartwood, it still has its uses. Just be certain to dry the sapwood thoroughly, and use it in projects where a little bit of movement will not cause problems, and where it will be thoroughly sealed (i.e. with paint) when finished.

Knots

A knot is a particular type of imperfection in a piece of timber, which reduces its strength but which may be exploited for artistic effect. A knot is actually a part of a side branch (or a dormant bud) included in the wood of the stem or larger branch.

Selecting a wood

The nature of the wood being carved limits the scope of the carver, in that wood is not equally strong in all directions. The direction in which wood is strongest is along the grain, whose pattern may be straight, interlocked, wavy or fiddle-back. It is wise to arrange the more delicate parts of a design along the grain instead of across it. Details designed in harmony with the growth of the wood and not too deeply undercut are more likely to remain intact.

Probably the most common woods used for carving are lime, sycamore, boxwood and cherry. These hardwoods are relatively easy to work with. Oak is a lovely wood for carving, durable and tough without being too hard. Chestnut (very like oak), American walnut, mahogany and teak are

Unicated rings, Kirsten Bak, 2005. Plane wood, plastic coating, 25 x 25 x 35 mm (1 x 1 x 1²/₅ in.). Photograph by Kirsten Bak.

also very good woods, while for fine work Italian walnut, sycamore, maple, apple, pear or plum are generally chosen. Decoration that is to be painted and is not too delicate is generally carved in pine.

Choosing the appropriate wood for carving can depend on many factors. Is the wood soft enough to cut easily with a knife, or do you need a chisel and mallet? Will it have a natural finish that shows the grain, or will it be painted?

Some makers choose interestingly shaped sticks or branches. A freshly cut piece of wood can present problems since it still contains a great deal of moisture. But if the wood dries too quickly it may check (crack) badly. To prevent this happening, it is best to let the wood air-dry for a period of time until it reaches an acceptable level of moisture content.

Basswood is a good choice for carving small objects or decorative designs on flat surfaces. It is soft and easy to carve, the close grain holds small carved detail, there are few knots or blemishes, and it is stable when dry. However, basswood's softness makes it difficult to apply a stain evenly on carved surfaces, or to attain a glossy finish. Most basswood carvings are painted.

For pieces with a natural wood finish, walnut, mahogany and cherry provide rich colour with an attractive grain pattern. Walnut, mahogany and cherry are rich in colour, moderately difficult to carve because of the dense grain, and they take finishes well. More work will be needed for these woods.

Safe carving:
- If you are using a chisel and chips are flying, or when using any power tool, wear safety glasses. Your eyes are your most valuable tool; protect them.
- If you are creating dust, be sure to wear a dust mask. Wood can contain toxic fungi, and some woods themselves can be hazardous.
- When applying force to push a tool through wood, you will find that it frequently slips. Always keep your hands behind the tool's sharp edge.

Curly brooch, Terhi Tolvanen, 2007. Silver, hazelnut wood, 14 cm (5½ in.).
Photograph by Francis Willemstijn.

Do not hold the wood in your lap while carving. Always try to secure the work piece on a table or in a vice so that both hands are free to control the tools. Cuts often happen when one hand is trying to hold the piece and the other hand is pushing hard on the tool – and it slips. Secure the work piece, and keep both hands on the tool and behind the sharp edge.

- Keep a well-equipped first-aid kit handy.

Carving:

- To carve efficiently, your tools must be razor-sharp. They should leave a shiny cut through the wood, with no white streaks to indicate a nick in the blade.
- To determine the direction of the grain, look at the long cell fibres. The darker streaks of the annual rings can help indicate the direction of the grain.

Sycamore wood sliced along the grain to illustrate the grain and ring patterns. Photograph by Beth Legg.

Kaire necklace, Kaire Rannik, 2006. Wood, silk, copper, silver, paint. 27 x 17 x 5 cm (10⅔ x 6⅔ x 2 in.). Photograph by Kaire Rannik.

- Carve in a downward direction onto the parallel lines of grain. Note that if the wood seems to be tearing, and your tools are sharp, then you are probably going in the wrong direction. If so, turn around and carve in the opposite direction.
- You can also carve diagonally across the grain and even parallel to it, but if you carve upwards against the grain, it will only tear and splinter the wood.

Using a knife:
- When working on a small carving that can be held in the hand, hold the wood in the left hand (assuming you are right-handed) and the knife in the right.
- Keep the left hand behind the knife and use the left thumb on the blunt side of the blade to act like a lever to control the cut. With the thumb stationary, rotate your right hand and wrist to make the cut. In this position, if the knife should slip, you will not be cut. The knife should never go flying off the wood. You can also hold the knife as though you were peeling an apple. Just be careful not to nick your thumb.

Roughing out:
- Remove as much of the scrap wood as possible with a piercing saw, and round out the basic shapes. This will help you to define the major planes of the object being carved.

Adding the details:

- After the structure has been established, you can begin to put in the details with the knife or files.
- At this point, it is important to keep tools razor-sharp if you intend to leave the tool marks as the final texture. Any nicks in the tool's edge will leave white lines in the tool's cut.

VEGETABLE IVORY

Vegetable ivory is obtained from the tagua or ivory-nut palm from the South American rainforest. It is often used to make beads and can also be dyed. It has similar properties to animal ivory and thus is sometimes used as a replica material; when dried out it can be carved. The ivory-nut palm is one of a number of palms whose seeds can be harvested for vegetable ivory.

JET

Jet is a variety of fossilised coal. A geological material not considered a mineral in the true sense of the word, jet is derived from decaying wood under extreme pressure, and thus is organic

Nut ring, An Alleweireldt, 2006. Vegetable ivory, 18 ct yellow gold. 4 x 5 cm (1½ x 2 in.). Photograph by An Alleweireldt.

in origin. Jet is black or dark brown but may contain pyrite inclusions, which have a brassy colour and a metallic lustre.

Anthracite (hard coal) and vulcanite are similar materials that have been used to imitate fine jet: these imitations are not always easy to distinguish from the real thing. Another similar material, black glass, is cool to the touch, unlike jet, which has greater insulating properties.

Jet as a gem material was highly popular during the reign of Queen Victoria, after the Queen herself wore Whitby jet as part of her mourning dress after the death of Prince Albert. Jet was popular for mourning jewellery in the 19th century because of its sombre colour and modest appearance, and has also been traditionally fashioned into rosaries for monks. However, in the United States in the 1920s, long necklaces of jet beads were very popular among the fashionable young women of the time, known as flappers, who wore multiple

FROM TOP: *Skyline* necklace, Evert Nijland, 2006. Ebony, silver, textile, length 50 cm (20 in). Photograph by Eddo Hartmann.

Abracadabra neckpiece, Caroline Holt, 2006. Silver, bone, jet, 2 x 3 cm (1¹/₂ x 2¹/₈ in.). Photograph by Caroline Holt.

Ring, Julie Mollenhauer, 2006. Amber. 2.7 x 3 x 0.5 cm (1 x 1⅕ x ⅕ in.). Photograph by Thomas Lenden.

strands stretching from the neck to the waistline. In these necklaces the jet was strung using heavy cotton thread; small knots were made on either side of each bead to keep the beads evenly spaced, much in the same way as fine pearl necklaces are made. Jet has also been known as black amber, as when rubbed it can induce an electric charge like that of amber. Powdered jet added to water or wine was once believed to have medicinal powers.

Jet is found in one of two forms, hard and soft. Hard jet is the result of the carbon compression and salt water; soft jet is the result of the carbon compression and fresh water.

AMBER

Amber is the common name for fossil resin. Most of the world's amber is in the range of 30 to 90 million years old. Amber is found along the shores of large parts of the Baltic and North Seas, but the main amber-producing country nowadays is Russia. Pieces of amber torn from the sea-floor are cast up by the waves and collected at ebb-tide.

Amber can be transparent, translucent or opaque, and of various colours. Despite being soft, it is considered to be a complicated material to work. Amber pieces come in a great range of shapes, and the process of grinding and polishing reveals a host of shades and textures, inclusions inside the piece, and some hardened semi-transparent clouds and air bubbles. A carved piece of amber catches and plays with light, and has a smooth, sensuous feel. It is soft (2–3 on the Mohs scale) and relatively easy to carve – you can use everyday tools and do it by hand, or use a flexible-shaft machine.

It is probably best to purchase amber from a reputable dealer, but when in doubt of its authenticity, there are a few ways to test amber to be sure it is not plastic. Firstly, in a spot you plan to carve away or hide, poke the material with a hot needle. Burning amber smells sweet and pine-like, not like plastic. Second, you can brush or soak it in methyl alcohol or ethyl acetate. Plastic will dissolve. (Caution: amber will dissolve in solvents like acetone or nail-polish remover.) Finally, you can mix 4 teaspoons of salt into an 8 oz glass of water. Real amber will float in it.

Amber resin often contains beautifully preserved plant structures and numerous remains of insects and other small organisms, called inclusions. In most cases the organic structure has disappeared, leaving only a cavity or bubble. Even hair and feathers have occasionally been represented among the enclosures. Fragments of wood frequently occur, with the tissues well-preserved by impregnation with the resin; while leaves, flowers and fruits are also occasionally found. Enclosures of iron pyrites may give a bluish colour to amber. The so-called black amber is actually a kind of jet, and bony amber owes its cloudy opacity to minute bubbles inside the resin. Even a strong wind might have affected the appearance of amber, by rippling the surface of a piece of resin that has not fully hardened. Semi-fossilised resin amber is called copal.

When gradually heated in an oil bath, amber becomes soft and flexible. Two pieces of amber may be joined by smearing the surfaces with linseed oil, heating them, and then pressing them together while hot. Cloudy amber may

Necklace, Julie Mollenhauer, 2006. Amber, silver. 18 x 18 x 1.5 cm (7 x 7 x ⅔ in.). Photograph by Thomas Lenden.

be clarified in an oil bath, as the oil fills the numerous pores which give rise to the cloudiness. Small fragments, formerly thrown away or used only for varnish, are now utilised on a large scale in the formation of amberoid or pressed amber. The pieces are carefully heated by excluding air and then compressed into a uniform mass under intense hydraulic pressure; the softened amber is forced through holes in a metal plate. The product is used extensively in the production of cheap jewellery. In that regard, true amber is sometimes coloured artificially.

Amber will soften if heated, and eventually it will burn. The aromatic and irritating fumes emitted by burning amber are mainly due to its acid content.

WORKING WITH AMBER

It always helps not to get too attached to a piece, because amber is brittle and can chip or break, and of course it cannot take heat. Look carefully at your amber, checking for any cracks, air bubbles or other areas you want to avoid or cut away. Initially, you may want to plan a fairly simple design.

Rough out the shape you want and take out spots you don't want, such as surface cracks. Start with rough sandpaper or sanding discs. Remember to have the amber and both hands well braced on the workbench for control. This is important for every stage of this kind of work.

Untitled necklace, Terhi Tolvanen, 2005, rosewood, silver, paint, glass, amber, 18 cm (7 in.) diameter. Photograph by Eddo Hartmann.

There are several types of cold connections which can be applied to amber. If you want your carving to be a pendant, for example, you could set the completed carving into a pendant with a bezel or claw-setting technique. Remember to be careful when bending the bezel or claws over the piece, as amber is soft and brittle.

However, if you want to drill through the piece and string or rivet it, it is always best to do so early on, before you've put too much time and energy into the carving, in case the amber shatters during drilling. Since most amber is transparent or semi-transparent, the hole you drill, and the element that goes through it, may be visible in your piece.

If you choose to drill into the piece, keep the burr speed slow enough so as not to burn the amber, work slowly and steadily, and keep the drill rotating. Continue drilling in and pulling out and blowing off dust. Don't stop in the middle or the drill will get stuck. If you are cutting or carving your design with a motorised drill, pay attention to the direction in which the burr moves, so you can spin it away from any edges and avoid chipping.

When finishing, sand the amber with finer and finer papers (higher grit numbers). Small pieces of sandpaper around toothpicks can get into hard to reach areas. After you've used 600-grit or finer, finish by rubbing the piece with brass polish on a soft cloth. Amber can also be turned on the lathe and polished with oil, the final lustre being given by friction with flannel.

LATEX

Latex, as found in nature, is the milky sap of plants or trees that coagulates upon exposure to air. Natural latex is mainly produced from the rubber tree *Hevea brasiliensis*. In most plants, latex is white, but in some it is yellow, orange or scarlet. It is believed that latex functions to protect the plant in case of injuries, drying to form a protective layer that prevents the entry of fungi and bacteria. Similarly, it may provide some protection against browsing animals, since in some plants the substance is very bitter or even poisonous. Latex is

collected by cutting a thin strip of bark from the tree and allowing the sap to ooze out into a collecting vessel over a period of hours. This laborious harvesting process meant that latex was once highly prized, and was even referred to as 'vegetable gold'.

Natural latex with a high solid content is also used for making moulds for casting plaster, cement, wax, low-temperature metals, and limited-run polyester articles. Natural latex has the ability to shrink around the object to be reproduced, so that the smallest detail will be repeated in the cast. Liquid latex can be used like paint, as well as layered, dyed and sewn into.

Necklace, Ela Bauer, 1995. Latex and fabric, 60 cm (23½ in.). Photograph by Ela Bauer.

9. Hair, Hides, Feathers and Wool

HIDES

Animal hides have provided an important source of clothing and shelter since prehistoric times. Hides are generally skins obtained from animals for human use. Examples of animal-hide sources are deer and cattle, typically used to produce leather; alligator skins and snake skins, used for shoes and fashion accessories; and wild cats, minks and bears, whose skins are primarily sought for their fur.

Animal hides have always been regarded as status symbols. Fur has always been used to demonstrate wealth, and leather is still used today in many expensive products.

RAWHIDE

Rawhide is a hide or animal skin that has not been exposed to tanning and thus is much lighter in colour than treated animal hides. Rawhide is made by scraping the skin thin, soaking it in lime, then stretching it while it dries. Rawhide is stiffer and more brittle than other forms of leather. The skin from buffalo, deer, elk or cattle, from which most rawhide originates, is devoid of all fur, meat and fat. The resulting material is often only semi-pliable and is also permeable to light. As such, it is considered suitable for use in objects ranging

Brooch, Jo Pond, 2005. Iron wire, silver, goatskin rawhide, 10 cm (4 in.). Photograph by Jo Pond.

from drumheads to lampshades. Wet rawhide shrinks significantly and strengthens tightly as it dries.

PARCHMENT

Parchment, a thin material made from calfskin, sheepskin or goatskin, was once commonly used in place of paper. Unlike leather, parchment is not tanned, but stretched, scraped and dried under tension, creating a stiff white, yellowish or translucent animal skin. Parchment is not waterproof, and thus is very reactive to changes in relative humidity, sometimes causing books with parchment pages to leap from library shelves. Today, true animal parchment is expensive and difficult to find; plant-based (vegetable) paper parchment is currently used as a substitute.

VELLUM

Vellum is a kind of parchment with finer qualities – thin, smooth and durable – a material traditionally used for the pages of a book. Strictly speaking, vellum should only be made from calfskin, but the term early on was used for the best quality of parchment, regardless of the animal from which the skin came. It is prepared essentially by soaking the skin in lime and drying it under tension. Nowadays, the most common kind of vellum is

Untitled, Sebastian Buescher, 2007. Earthenware, silver, vellum, galvanised steel, gold, plastic, 8 x 5 cm (2³/₄ x 2 in.). Photograph by Sebastian Buescher.

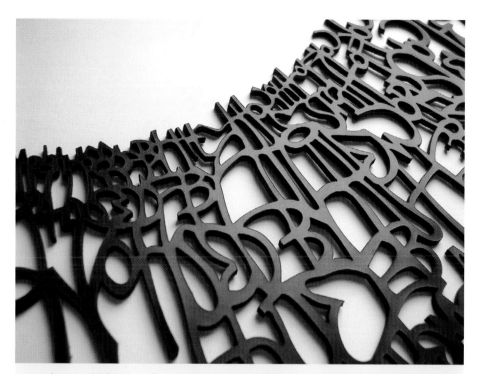

Leather Scribble (detail), Laura Bezant, 2006. Laser-cut leather. Photograph by Laura Bezant.

a modern imitation made out of cotton, although a small amount of true vellum is still made. Vellum can be stained virtually any colour but seldom is, as a great part of its beauty and appeal rests in its faint grain and hair markings, as well as its warmth and simplicity.

LEATHER

There are a number of processes whereby the skin of a dead animal can be formed into the supple, strong material commonly known as leather. The leather production process generally involves steps like soaking, liming, dehairing, de-liming, degreasing, bating, pickling, tanning, dyeing and finishing.

The natural fibres of leather will break down with the passage of time. Acidic leathers are particularly vulnerable to red rot, which causes powdering of the surface and a change in consistency. Damage from red rot is aggravated by high temperatures and relative humidity, and is irreversible. Exposure to long periods of low relative humidity can cause leather to become desiccated, irreversibly changing the fibrous structure of the leather.

'Listen' Brooch, Iris Eichenberg.
Silver, hair. 14 x 4 cm (5½ x 1½ in.).
Photograph by Ron Zijlstra.

Various treatments are available, such as conditioners, but these are not recommended by conservators since they impregnate the structure of the leather artefact with active chemicals, are sticky, and attract stains.

Vegetable-tanned leather, can be oiled to improve its water-resistance. This supplements the natural oils remaining in the leather itself, which will tend to be washed out through repeated exposure to water. Frequent oiling of leather with neatsfoot oil or a similar material keeps it supple and improves its lifespan dramatically.

HAIR

The special qualities of hair as a medium for remembrance lie in its narrative implications: its cut ends refer to the absent body. The forming and framing of hair in mourning jewels both reflects and creates tensions between presence and absence, and between revealing and hiding.

WOOL

Wool is the fibre derived principally from sheep, but the hair of certain species of other mammals such as goats, alpacas, llamas and rabbits may also be called wool. Wool has two qualities that distinguish it from hair or fur: it has scales which overlap like slates on a roof, and it is crimped; in some fleeces the wool fibres have more than 20 bends, or crimps, per inch.

Dyed felting wool fleece. Available in a wide range of colours or undyed, felting wool is pre-washed and carded, or brushed straight.

Katharina Collier, Constanze Schreiber, 2005. Fur, lead, silver, 42 x 25 x 2 cm (15³/₄ x 10 x ³/₄ in.). Photograph by Edo Kuipers.

Wool's scaling and crimp make it easier to spin and felt the fleece. They help the individual fibres attach to each other so that they stay together. Because of the crimp, wool fabrics have a greater bulk than other textiles, and retain air, causing the product to retain heat. But insulation also works both ways: Bedouins and Tuaregs use wool clothes to keep the heat out.

The amount of crimp corresponds to the thickness of the wool fibres. A fine wool like merino may have up to a hundred crimps per inch, while the coarser wools like karakul may have as few as one or two crimps per inch.

Hair, by contrast, has little if any scale and no crimp, and little ability to bind into yarn. On sheep, the hair part of the fleece is called kemp. The relative amounts of kemp to wool vary from breed to breed, and make some fleeces more desirable for spinning, felting or carding into batts for quilts or other insulating products.

Wool is generally a creamy-white colour, although some breeds of sheep produce natural colours such as black, brown (also called moorit) and grey. Wool readily takes dyes.

Nieuw Work Brooch, Iris Eichenberg. Silver, wool, porcelain, medical or dental plastic. 12 x 12 cm (4¾ x 4¾ in.). Photograph by Ron Zijlstra.

FELTING

Felting is the earliest textile-making technique with symbolic associations with nomadic culture, where it originated. Felt is a non-woven cloth produced by matting, condensing and pressing fibres. The fibres form the structure of the fabric, so it is very soft. Felt is made of wool compressed by heat and agitation. The process of felting needs very few aids and thus is not bound to a particular place.

Felted sheet – different colours of fleece can be layered and fused together at different thicknesses.

Felt is a very versatile material – it can be dense and rigid or light and flexible. An adaptable and practical material, it conjures strong ideas of protection and warmth, though it is just as good in protecting against extreme heat.

When planning a project, remember that felt will shrink in size, so you will need to make allowances. For example, a 60 cm (24 in.) square will shrink a little less than 20% to a finished size of approximately 50 cm (20 in.). To make a 50 cm (20 in.) square piece of felt, you will need approximately 5–6 oz of pure wool fleece.

Materials
- An old sock
- A bowl of cold water and ice cubes
- A tray (to catch excess water)
- A sponge (to sop up the water so it can be reheated)
- Kitchen scales (To make balls of a uniform size, you'll need to weigh the wool before you start.)
- Felting wool
- A bowl of hot soapy water (A formula of 4 tablespoons of liquid detergent to 6 cups of water enables the wool fibres to cling together and become felt. It's best to use detergent that does not contain scents or dyes.)

FELT BALLS

Step 1
To get started, pull out a wad of the wool. The wool compacts, so get a wad slightly bigger than you want your finished bead to be. Pull the wool apart to untangle it. NB *It is important to pull off pieces and not to cut the wool.*

Step 2
Fill up one basin with hot water – as hot as you can stand. Add some washing-up liquid to it and froth it up to dissolve the soap. Put water and ice cubes in the other basin. You will need these two basins because the felting of the wool will occur when the wool is exposed to friction and temperature changes. The wool fibres will shrink up – this is a permanent action. When you roll the wool between your palms and alternate between the hot and cold basins (in steps 3 and 4), the wool will felt to itself and shrink into a ball, which you will shape as you work with it.

Step 3
Immerse the wool you pulled off into the hot water basin, and then rub it vigorously between your palms, the way you might roll clay to make a round ball. After a few seconds, immerse the wool in the cold water and then continue to roll it between your palms.

Step 4
You will see and feel the wool begin to tighten into a ball. Continue alternating between the hot and cold baths, rolling the wool in your hands, until a very compact bead is formed.

Step 5
To finish the beads, put them in the sock and dry them in the dryer for 30 minutes. The heat of the dryer will continue to shrink the wool. If you don't have access to a dryer you can put the balls in a washing machine on a fast spin, which will help to felt them further and rid them of excess water. They can then be dried in an airing cupboard or on a radiator. When the beads are dry, you can sew through them or onto their surfaces using embroidery threads and beads. A few beads can be strung together to make a necklace by pushing a long needle right through the centre of the bead.

FELT JUMP RINGS (HOOPS)

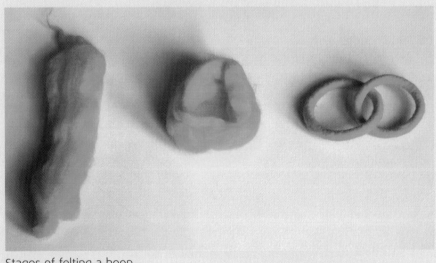

Stages of felting a hoop.

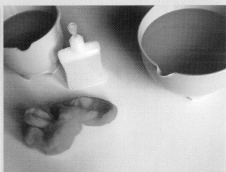

Step 1
Measure the circumference needed for your hoop. Pull off a piece of wool approximately 50% longer than you need (the wool shrinks by approximately 50%), i.e. if you want your link to be 20 cm (8 in.) long, add 10 cm (4 in.) extra. If you want to make a thick hoop, pull off a wide piece of wool. Lay it out as a ring, ensuring the ends overlap and the thickness is even.

Step 2
Holding the join firmly, dip the whole ring in a bowl of warm soapy water. When the whole ring is wet, remove it and add a little soap to the join. Lightly massage the soap into the wool with your fingers. When you feel the ends have joined, dip the ring in again and squeeze out.

Step 3
Hold the ring between your palms and carefully roll it back and forth. Dip again, squeeze out

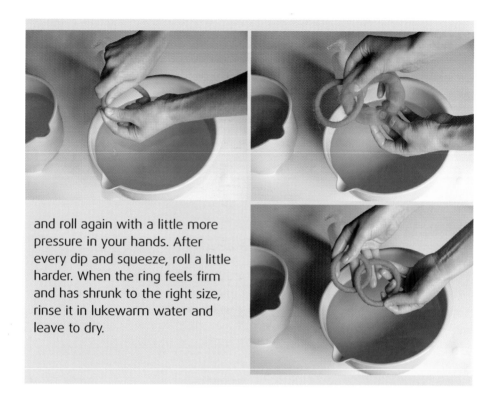

and roll again with a little more pressure in your hands. After every dip and squeeze, roll a little harder. When the ring feels firm and has shrunk to the right size, rinse it in lukewarm water and leave to dry.

FEATHERS

Feathers have obvious appeal as immediate tools of texture, colour and form, but also as symbols of flight and otherworldliness. The idea of employing feathers for personal adornment is as ancient as early humanity's interest in self-decoration, and plumage, as the by-product of a food source, has always been readily available.

Feathers are among the most complex structural organs found in vertebrates. They insulate birds from water and cold temperatures, while individual feathers in the wings and tail play important roles in controlling flight. Although feathers are light, a bird's plumage weighs two or three times more than its skeleton, since many bones are hollow and contain air sacs.

In jewellery, the texture, lightness, colour and mobility of feathers make an interesting juxtaposition with elements made in metal. The flexibility and structure of a feather allows it to be used in many ways.

Working with Feathers

Quills can be pierced very simply by heating the point of a needle or wire of appropriate thickness then pressing it through. They can then be threaded and strung on nylon or wire. This manner of mounting feathers can be flat in a series or several feathers tied together in groups to create dimensional forms and bunches.

Groups of feathers can also be bonded together using an adhesive, and the ends of the quills can be bound together, for example, with silk thread. The adhesive used on feathers should be non-permanent and water-soluble in order that it doesn't corrode or discolour the barbs.

In order to cut feathers to shape you should glue them individually onto card with water-soluble glue. Once the glue has dried, cut the feather to shape using very sharp scissors or a new scalpel blade. The card will help you cut accurately and keep the barbs together for a sharp line. Once you have cut the feather, soak the glue from the cardboard and peel away your cut feather.

Trace feather wrap, Anna Lewis, 2003. Printed feathers, crin & millinery wire, 40 x 50 cm (16 x 20 in.). Photograph by Anna Lewis.

Peewit-feather rings, Beth Legg, 2003. Silver & found feather in glass petri dish, 10 cm (4 in.). Photograph by John K. MacGregor.

Vanished feather wrap, Anna Lewis, 2003. Printed feathers and thread, 150 x 30 cm (60 x 12 in.). Photograph by Jesse Seaward.

10. Cold Connections

In the jewellery world the term 'cold connections' usually describes mechanical joining techniques used to fasten together parts that cannot be soldered (by using a 'hot' connection). It's worth noting that claw, prong and bezel settings also belong in the cold-connection category. In many cases, cold connections fall into a 'layer this onto that' approach. Cold connections are more than a range of techniques: they can trigger new ways to think about design. By combining function, engineering and aesthetics, cold connections can lead us to fresh ideas.

RIVETING

If you cannot solder or don't want to solder two elements together then riveting is one of the most secure and useful cold-connection techniques. For this reason it is a particularly successful process for working with natural materials. Riveting involves fitting a wire or tube through a tight hole and then splaying the ends until the components are securely held together. Put basically, rivets are like a two-headed nail. The rivets used can be either almost completely invisible, or have obvious heads, in various shapes, that become intrinsic elements in the aesthetics of a piece.

Northsea brooch, Francis Willemstijn, 2004. Silver, gold, ebony. Approx. 9 x 5 x 3 cm (3½ x 2 x 1⅛ in.). Photograph by Francis Willemstijn.

Untitled brooch, Joe Sheehan, 2005. New Zealand jade, white enamel paint and silver, 5.5 cm x 6.5 cm ($2^1/_8$ x $2^1/_2$ in.). Photograph by Joe Sheehan.

When using rivets for your design, it is often best to think and draw out your design beforehand to make best use of the rivets as part of the design. Consider the ergonomics of the finished piece – whether you want any movement in the rivets and how visible you would like them to be.

Rivets can be bought with rounded heads, or you can make your own by balling the end of a wire with the fine flame of a blowtorch. To work with these rivets it is best to use special riveting tools; these resemble punches, with domed depressions the size of the rivet head in one end. The following example involves a similar process but only requires a basic toolkit and doming punches.

Note that if you are riveting a brittle natural material such as shell, be very careful not to hammer too hard – set up as much protection around the piece as possible using scraps of leather, etc.

TUBE RIVETING

Equipment
- Basic toolkit
- Vice
- Ball peen or repoussé hammer
- Drill (electric or hand)
- Steel doming punch
- Annealed section of silver tube (or wire for wire riveting)
- Safety glasses (if you are using an electric drill)

1. Mark the top piece of material with a pencil or marker where you want to drill the holes to place the rivets. Place a steel punch on the mark you've made and tap it with your hammer to make an indentation. This is done so that when you place the drill bit on the metal and begin to drill, it has a place to sit and won't skitter across the surface, scratching your piece or snapping the bit.

2. Drill a hole the same diameter as the outside diameter of the tube through the material you have chosen to work with, so that the tube fits snugly. Sometimes with the right design you can tape the two pieces together, because it is easier to drill both pieces at the same time. This is a good way of keeping your holes accurate.

3. Saw the tube to the correct length – it should be slightly longer than the width of the two elements you are joining, giving just under a 1 mm protrusion on either side.

4. Place a domed punch, slightly larger than the diameter of the tube, in the vice. The tube is rested on the punch and another round-ended punch or centre punch is hammered onto the other end of the tube in order to splay the rivet.

5. Turn the piece over and repeat this process on the other side. The ball end of a hammer can be used to flatten off the rivet.

6. Tidy up any rough edges or burrs with emery paper.

A variation on this rivet is to saw down the two ends of the tube before riveting, so that when it is hammered the tube will splay out into two separate petal-like shapes.

WIRE-RIVETING

Wire-riveting involves exactly the same process and tools as tube-riveting except that in stage 4 you should take the ball end of your hammer and gently tap the edges of the end of the wire in a circle. You keep doing this until you see a head develop on the end of the wire. If you hit the wire too hard it will bend – you don't want to bend the wire; you want to stretch it so that it forms a flat head. If you then use a flat-headed hammer and file down the wire, you should achieve a flush and almost invisible rivet.

Note that if there is to be more than one rivet on a piece then care has to be taken to ensure all holes line up on both elements. It might be useful to drill all the holes through the top piece with only one hole continuing through to the bottom piece. Rivet this hole securely and then drill the other holes right through the bottom piece and rivet.

Riveting can be a very successful mechanism for allowing movement. If there is a slight looseness or gap, a pivoting motion can be achieved. A gap can be made between two connected parts by riveting cardboard or thick paper between them. The thicker the cardboard the more play you will have between the two pieces. This can be soaked out once the rivet has been completed. For a wider gap, or to prevent two parts rubbing, a length of tube can be slipped over the rivet between the two connected parts.

Finally, be aware that riveting can be awkward and might require an extra pair of hands.

Eda brooch, Ketli Tiitsar, 2005.
Black wood & oxidised silver,
3.5 x 5 cm (1³/₈ x 2 in.).
Photograph by Ketli Tiitsar.

Untitled brooch, Lucy Sarneel, 2003. Red gold, plastic, ice-lolly sticks, silver, shells filled with epoxy. Approx. 9 x 5 x 2.5 cm (3½ x 2 x 1 in.). Photograph by Ron Zijlstra.

SETTING

This is one of the most commonly used and effective forms of cold connection. In this process the jewellery piece is always completed with the setting in position before the natural element is set in place. The kind of material you are working with might dictate the type of setting you apply. The level of protection required for your set element should be taken into account: for example, a piece of wood might be quite soft, whereas slate or a pebble might be much more resilient. Some materials, such as thin shell or amber, might gain from a more protective setting such as a bezel. The hardness of your natural object needs to be kept in mind at all times when setting – especially at the stage of using metal tools to set the object.

BEZEL-SETTING

The bezel or rub-over setting is probably the simplest to apply and is traditionally used on cabochon-cut stones but can be very effective when applied to natural objects. In this form of setting the object rests on a wire or ledge inside the bezel or on the base sheet of metal the bezel is soldered to. When the object is fitted into the bezel, the very top of the metal wall is pushed against the side or edge of the object to hold it in place. Bezel strips of fine gold or silver can be bought from most metal suppliers, but you can also use metal from your own stock if it is cut or rolled into thin strips and is thin enough to be pushed over an object.

Equipment
- Basic toolkit
- Bezel strip or thin sheet strip in metal of your choice
- Setting tool
- Burnisher

1. Take your bezel strip (no wider than the height of the object you are setting) and cut it to the correct length. To help you calculate this length there are equations for regular shapes such as circles, but when working with natural, irregular objects it is easiest to wrap masking tape around the circumference of the object and mark on the tape where it meets. Lay the tape out flat, measure it and add the thickness of your bezel strip to this number, and you have your required length. You can also do this with the bezel strip itself.

2. Ensure the ends of your bezel are neat, then test the bezel size on your object before soldering the ends together.

3. If the bezel appears to fit and the ends are clean and have no gaps, solder them together using a very small amount of hard solder.

4. Once the setting is soldered and pickled clean, it is shaped to fit the object. At this stage ensure that the object fits snugly: it should not be loose and should drop into the bezel without being forced. If your object has an uneven base, you might need to sand or cut it flat before adjusting the bezel wall height.

5. Now that the setting fits, emery the base and top of the bezel so that it sits flat.

At this point check that the bezel is high enough to secure the object but not too high. Lay the object and the setting on a flat surface to judge the correct height, and rub away any excess metal if necessary.

6. Check that the setting is still the right shape for your object and then solder it onto a base sheet of metal slightly larger than your setting – I am using 0.6 mm silver sheet – then pickle clean.

7. Remove any excess edges around the setting by sawing or filing, then emery. Unless you want to keep an edge, saw as close to the solder line as possible without touching the setting itself.

8. If you want to test the fit of your object at this stage, apply beeswax or Blu-Tack to some dowelling or the end of a pencil; this can be placed on top of your object, allowing you to lift it in and out of the setting with ease.

Untitled necklace, Terhi Tolvanen, 2004. Hazelnut wood, silver, jade, 18 cm (7¹/₈ in.). Photograph by Eddo Hartmann.

9. At this stage you can apply your chosen fittings to the setting depending on whether you want your setting to be part of a brooch, necklace, etc.

10. Prepare the bezel for setting the object by ensuring that there are no filings or other obstructions, such as excess solder, on the inside of the bezel, and that you have obtained your chosen finish on all metal parts.

11. It is important to gain a good grip on the piece when setting. A ring may be held in a clamp or a brooch rested on a block of wood where the settings can rest over the edge. Every piece is different – you just need to find which way is best for working on each setting.

12. Using an appropriate stone setting tool that has a polished end so that it doesn't mark the object or setting, push the metal over onto the object.

Position the pushing tool against the bezel at about 45° to 50° toward the top of the bezel, and push the bezel toward the object. Begin by pushing the bezel toward the object from one direction, then rotate to the opposite side and repeat.

Move the bezel around by 90° from the previous location and push that area toward the object. Work evenly around the setting, in this way ensuring full contact between the natural object and the metal.

13. If you have achieved good and full contact during the pushing process, there might be no need to burnish the bezel. If there are small gaps that just won't 'push' against the object, burnishing is the best way to finish the process.

14. Only minor finishing work is required if you are careful with the pushing process. If necessary, use an escapement file or emery to remove setting marks.

LEDGE-SETTING

Ledge bezel-setting is when the element rests on an inner ledge rather than a backplate. This allows the piece to be set up high or have an open base that lets light in.

Shetland Pebble brooch, Grace Girvan, 2006. Silver, pebbles, wood, 6 x 5.5 cm (2³/₈ x 2¹/₈ in.). Photograph by Grace Girvan.

To make a ledge setting, follow the same initial process of making a bezel to snugly fit your element and then do the same with a narrower bezel that fits snugly inside the first. This is the ledge. Push the two bezels together so that the base rims are flush. The top of the outside bezel should be higher than the inner one – allowing the metal to be pushed over the piece, completing the setting.

If this setting has a backplate then there is no need to solder the inner ledge in place.

CLAW- OR PRONG-SETTING

This form of setting allows the maximum amount of light into the piece. Claw settings for traditionally cut stones can be bought as castings from suppliers, but the irregular shapes and angles of natural objects mean it is most likely you will have to custom-make a setting from scratch yourself.

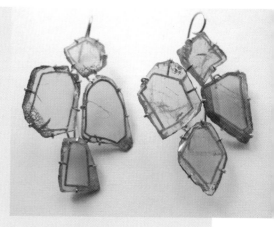

Earrings, Bettina Speckner, 2006. Gold 750 & titanite or 'sphene', 5.5 cm (2¹⁄₈ in.). Photograph by Bettina Speckner.

The setting process is easier than with a bezel because there is less metal to be moved, but it is more tricky to fabricate the setting itself. This can be constructed from pierced-out sheet or wire, while the prongs can be in round, square, rectangular or triangular sections and are sometimes tapered at the claw.

These forms of open settings can be made incorporating a bezel like the ones already discussed, where the prongs are cut into the setting and then bent back. Another variation on this involves soldering wire prongs around the outer edge of the bezel.

After any last burrs or flaws in the mounting have been removed, the natural object is pressed into position and checked to see that it touches each prong. If not it is removed and the prongs adjusted accordingly. The prongs are next checked to ensure they are the proper height, and if

Earrings, Bettina Speckner, 2006. Photo in enamel, silver, red gold, ammonite, 5.5 x 2 cm (2¹⁄₈ x ³⁄₄ in.). Photograph by Bettina Speckner.

necessary cut down and shaped with files. Each prong is then pressed over the object part-way, the object is checked to ensure it is level, and the prongs are set down firmly onto the the object. The tips of each prong are hardened and burnished with a burnisher.

Rings, Sarah King. African blackwood & silver. 3 x 2.5 x 1.5 cm (1⅛ x 1 x ⅔ in.). Photograph by Sarah King. Inlay technique – the wood is carved into shape and the channel is drilled using a pendant drill and round burr.

INLAY

The traditional inlay technique, in which contrasting metals are placed side by side, involves the process of securing a soft material into a harder one. This form of metal inlay requires materials of contrasting hardness to hold well, and contrasting colour to look good.

In natural material inlay, the principals are very similar: stone, wood or shells are cut to fit snugly within the recesses of a setting, or alternatively the setting is itself of natural material and metal sheet or wire is set into this. The inlay is usually flush with the surface, although it is possible for the object to be in relief. You should, however, bear in mind the fragility of the inlay if it is intended to sit proud of its setting.

Particularly fine examples of natural material inlay can be seen in the work of Native American artists. They cut and polish stones (usually turquoise), then arrange them in plaques that are recesses defined by thick-walled bezels. The plaques themselves often have intriguing shapes depicting animals, geometric forms, even landscapes. Almost any type of stone or other hard, organic material can be used for inlay as long as you can extract a flattish sheet from it. The most common materials, however, are turquoise, coral, onyx and mother-of-pearl shell.

PLAQUE INLAY

Plaque inlay is quite similar to bezel-setting. A metal border surrounds the inlaid object, but there is no rub-over: the natural material is set flush with the thickly walled setting and held in place with adhesive. The basic techniques of plaque inlay are pretty easy to learn and probably the best inlay application for a novice to try. This process will walk you through the fundamentals of shell inlay until that you become comfortable enough to move on to more challenging projects. The contrasting colours, qualities and textures that can be achieved also make this an appealing technique.

Equipment
- Basic toolkit
- Safety goggles, dust mask, apron
- Emery papers of decreasing grades
- Mother-of-pearl shell or any 'sheet' of shell of your choice
- Two-part epoxy adhesive
- Scrap wood
- Wooden dowels (thin)
- Charcoal stick or colour pastels (optional)
- Cardboard or cardstock (optional)
- Coloured paper (optional)
- Dental floss (optional)

1. To fabricate a plaque, cut a piece of square-section wire to your desired plaque length and size – for this setting I have used 0.8 mm ($^5/_{16}$ in) gauge rolled flat. Bring the ends of the wire together to form a border, and solder the seam using hard solder. Pickle, then rinse in water.

2. Form the border to your desired shape.

Step 1

Step 2

3. Pierce out a piece of silver sheet metal – I have used 0.6 mm thickness – to the size of the border.

4. Solder the border to the sheet metal using small pieces of solder. Pickle the plaque, rinse and dry it. Use a jeweller's saw or file to tidy around its perimeter, forming a cup. Emery the cut edge until it is smooth.

Step 4

5. This is the point where you can join the plaque to your piece of jewellery. This can be soldered onto a pre-prepared brooch, for example, or onto jump rings for securing to a bracelet or necklace. Bear in mind that you'll be custom-cutting shell to fit each plaque.

Step 6

6. Scribe or mark the shell pieces into the shape of your setting. If you are making a regular shape such as a circle, you can measure the interior circumference of the plaques. Using a scribe or pencil, draw a shape with the same circumference or shape onto the face of the shell pieces. Alternatively, you can make a template out of cardboard and test it in your setting, and then scribe onto your shell – particularly useful if you are doing repeats.

Step 7

7. Cut the shell into workable pieces. If the shell is a large slab

Step 8

or chunk, use a trim saw to slice off manageable pieces close to the size of your plaques.

8. Cut the shell to size using a piercing saw. It is important to keep the blade and shell pieces wet while cutting.

9. Continuing to work wet, sand the back of the shell piece flat if it isn't already so. You can do this with emery or wet-and-dry papers taped to a flat surface such as a steel block.

10. When a rough shape has been properly achieved, dry the piece before filing.

11. Hold the shell perpendicular to your file and rotate it frequently in your hand to grind away everything just outside of your scribed line. Frequently test the shell for its fit in the plaque and continue filing until it fits snugly. You can lay a length of string or dental floss under your shell if it is snug in the plaque, to help you release it later if need be.

12. Prepare your tools and materials for setting. Epoxy dries fast, so prepare your work area with all the materials you'll need: your plaque, shell piece, scribe, two-part epoxy, scrap wood, charcoal (optional) and thin wooden dowels. If you are

Step 9

Step 10

Step 12

Ensure you have as good a fit as possible before mixing your adhesive.

working on a few settings, place each shell piece next to its respective plaque so you can work quickly once the epoxy is mixed.

13. Score the plaque bed. Use a scribe to score the plaque bed (not the walls). This will give the epoxy a rough surface to adhere to.

Step 13

14. Set the shell piece. Squeeze equal-sized portions of the two epoxy parts onto a scrap piece of wood, and mix the parts together. You can add charcoal powder or coloured-pastel powder to the epoxy to enhance the shell's appearance after setting – I have oxidised my silver instead.

15. Apply the adhesive mixture to the inside of a plaque using the dowel.

Step 15

16. Press a shell piece into the plaque, and use another dowel to lightly tap it into place.

17. Repeat this process for each of your plaques if you are setting a series. Remember to work quickly, as epoxy dries fast. Allow the pieces to dry for at least an hour or, even better, overnight.

Step 16

18. If you need to, emery the shell down so that it is flush with the plaque; this can be done in a similar way to the earlier method of using emery or wet-and-dry papers taped to a flat surface.

19. As you go down the grades of paper you will polish the shell surfaces. Rinse the shell in water between papers.

20. Polish the plaque and burnish the edges if required.

TINTED SETTINGS

When setting shell or other objects, bear in mind that the colour of the plaque's interior often affects the shell's appearance, depending on the type of shell or stone used. Black coloration beneath mother-of-pearl shell gives the shell's surface a grey, blue and purple haze. A fine, black colouring pigment can be produced by rubbing a wooden dowel against a charcoal stick. Grate the charcoal powder directly into your epoxy, and mix it in. Grating coloured pastels into your epoxy will do the same job. Coat the lining of your plaque with the coloured adhesive, then set your shell or other object.

CREATING CAVITIES

The principle behind metal inlays is that wire or pieces of sheet are forced into cavities or hollowed-out areas. These are cut so that their walls flare inwards or are 'undercut', thus ensuring that a piece of metal will get stuck there once it is forcibly rammed in. It is a simple process and, given that inlays still exist which are many hundreds of years old, an effective one. While the pressing-in requires sensitive hammering, the most important part of inlay work lies in cutting the cavity in the first place. There are several methods available to a maker.

Rings, Sarah King, African blackwood & freshwater pearls. 4 x 2.5 x 1.8 cm (1½ x 1 x ¾ in.). Photograph by Sarah King. The pearls have been set in a cup, which was drilled with a round burr on the pendant drill before a small hole was drilled into the centre of the base of the cup. A silver peg, or post, is glued down into this central hole and into another one in the pearl.

Burring or milling

In a miniature milling operation, a burr can be used in the flexible shaft machine or pillar drill to remove metal. Once the cavity has been excavated with a ball, barrel or similar burr, the walls can be given the necessary undercut with an inverted cone burr or with a narrow graver.

Each piece will demand a new approach, so it is best to let your instincts guide you. The point is to create a cavity with sharp edges, a uniform depth, and walls.

Engraving

An ideal approach for delicate linear designs is to make a pair of cuts with a narrow graver. This tool is driven along a drawn line at a steep angle; the same tool is then passed along the same line at the opposite slant, creating a cavity with a swallow-tailed cross section. In cases where the desired inlay is larger than the width of a wire, sheet material is used. In these cases, a square graver is used to excavate the area.

Chiselling

Using chisels to cut away sections of metal sheet is an effective technique that has the advantage of being relatively easy to learn. The metal is secured on pitch as for repoussé, or in some similar way clamped onto a sturdy work surface. Chisels of several sizes and shapes will probably be needed. The tool is held between the thumb and the first two fingers and struck lightly with a small hammer. Particularly when first learning this technique, beware of gouging out too much at a time; think of shaving off layers of metal until the proper depth is reached. The cavity should have smooth walls and a flat bottom and attain a uniform depth throughout.

Using punches

This method is similar to chiselling except that no metal is removed. Thus it is not recommended for large inlays, though it can be very efficient for small wires. Select a sharp-lined punch tool that will cast up a burr on both sides of its mark. Use magnification to check the results of the indentation.

Follow the first indentation with another punch, this time a flat-ended one that will widen the groove to accept the inlay. Only a small amount of metal is needed to secure the wire, but it must stand up above the surface. It is important to select tools of the proper size and to strike each blow cleanly so that the tiny burr is not accidentally pressed down.

Fern brooch, Beth Legg, 2007.
Silver & burnt rose (wood).
Approx 12 cm long. Photograph
by Beth Legg.

FIXING THE INLAY IN PLACE

Wire inlay into undercuts
Use an annealed wire that is a proper fit for the groove. A wire that is too small will not be securely held, while an oversize wire risks distorting the inlay (as well as requiring tedious extra finishing). Start at one end of the groove, tapping the wire lightly into place for a short distance, then proceed to the next area. The idea is to press the wire outwards into the swallowtail or undercut area, locking it into place. The action has the added advantage of work-hardening the inlay.

Once the wire is firmly pressed into place, use a smooth-faced planishing punch to even the surface and refine the inlay. Make a series of light passes over the wire and its edges, feathering the surface until it is flush.

Relief inlays
While most inlays are flush, it is also possible to create an inlay that stands above the surface of the base. In the case of sheet inlays, the piece might be formed through repoussé or casting. The inlay process is the same as described above, but of course the inlay panel must not be planished. Instead

it is pressed flat with carefully located punches that will not damage the shape of the panel.

Make sure that:

- The natural and metal materials are free of tool marks, scratches and abrasions.
- The natural material inlay fits precisely into the channel, and no gaps or filler materials are visible.
- The natural material inlay is appropriately thick, solid and substantial. It has no cracks and is in full contact with the channel walls and bottom surface.

ADHESIVE BONDING

Available in a wide variety of formulas, epoxy resins are used in jewellery-making as adhesives, as coatings, and for casting. Epoxy resins are available at craft and art-supply stores as well as from online suppliers. The two-part formula has a liquid hardener that is added to a liquid resin and mixed to yield an epoxy resin that is easy to pour into bezels, moulds and forms. The adhesive does not become active until equal amounts are mixed together to form a thick viscous adhesive. In small quantities it is sold in tubes or syringes, in larger quantities in metal tins. Trade names include Araldite, Devcon, Humbrol Super Fast Epoxy and Permabond. Care should be taken in selecting the right epoxy for the job based upon the curing times. For most purposes, a five-minute resin offers rapid construction whilst allowing for small adjustments. On large areas that can be held in position epoxy resins that cure in 12 to 24 hours offer a tremendously strong bond.

Superglue

Superglue can be used in most situations to obtain a fast strong bond between components; 'slow'-setting superglue is recommended for a stronger bond. When using epoxy resins try to trim away any excess adhesive prior to curing. Just before the glue sets it can be trimmed with a sharp blade.

Air-bubble holes in some resin parts can be filled using fast-setting epoxy resin. Clean before the full cure is achieved and then sand back to the required profile.

When using superglue never apply the glue directly to the part. Always place the glue onto a waste piece and apply with a small disposable tool to avoid excessive amounts covering the piece.

Types of epoxy resin

Epoxy adhesives can be developed that meet almost any application. They are exceptional adhesives for wood, metal, glass, stone and some plastics. They can be made flexible or rigid, transparent or opaque/coloured, fast-setting or extremely slow.

Epoxy resins originally developed as adhesives, such as Araldite, harden quickly. They are used primarily for stone inlay but can also be used for coating applications. The drawbacks to working with epoxy adhesives are their strong chemical odour and short cure time.

Epoxy resins used for coating are less viscous formulations, and have a longer cure time, than adhesive epoxy resins. These products are self-levelling and yield a smooth, glasslike surface after they are cured. Casting epoxy resins can be poured into moulds to create three-dimensional plastic objects that could be used to trap and encase objects.

Safety with epoxy resin

The best safety precaution you can take when using any epoxy is to read all safety instructions that accompany the product. The product packaging may also list a Web address with additional downloadable safety guidelines and information. Most epoxy resins are non-toxic, organic compounds that, once cured, do not irritate the skin. However, in the liquid state, both the resins and hardeners are skin and eye irritants. It is good practice to wear protective gloves and safety glasses and to work in a well-ventilated space when using epoxy resins. Always handle with care, and follow the proper use and disposal methods recommended by the manufacturer.

If you plan to use these materials regularly or advance to plastic casting using polyester resins, buy a respirator with the correct filters for the chemicals you will be using.

Working with epoxy resin

Epoxy resins come in two parts: resin and hardener. The two parts must be mixed in the precise ratio given in the manufacturer's instructions. Imprecise measuring and mixing prevents the epoxy resin from solidifying or curing.

To mix small amounts of one-to-one formulas, it can be helpful to create a mixing template on a piece of cardboard. Draw two small, equal-sized circles on the cardboard. Place a piece of waxed paper over the cardboard, then fill one circle with resin and the other with hardener. Use a toothpick or similar to slowly and thoroughly mix the two parts.

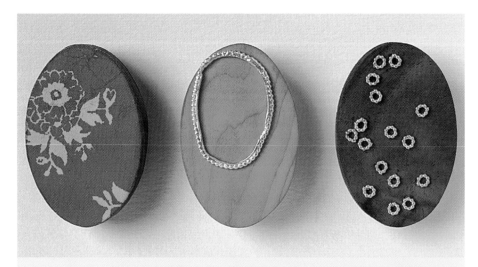

Three wooden brooches, Alison Macleod, 2005. 5 x 3.5 cm (2 x 1⅜ in.).
Walnut, yew, vintage wallpaper and silver. Photograph by John K. MacGregor.

When mixing large quantities or when incorporating colour additives, you could use a digital scale to weigh the resin and hardener to ensure that you achieve the measurements called for by the manufacturer. Note that some liquid colouring agents must be weighed with the resin to calculate the proper ratio of resin to hardener.

Different brands of epoxy resin have different lengths of curing time and 'pot life'. 'Pot life' refers to the amount of time during which you can pour or work with the epoxy before it starts to thicken. Curing time is the time it takes the epoxy to reach its full hardness and be dry to the touch. Adhesive epoxy resins generally have a short pot life and curing time, which makes it challenging to fill a mould and remove any air bubbles before the resin begins to thicken. Coating epoxy resins have a longer pot life and curing time. Select an epoxy resin with the pot life and curing time that will allow you to get the results you want.

Bear in mind that vigorously mixing the resin and hardener will produce air bubbles. To pop the bubbles, exhale on them, pierce them with a pin, or pass a heat gun set on 'low' over the surface of the epoxy resin.

PINNING

Pinning, or using a post, is the most basic manner of attaching a natural material to a metal body piece, and also allows for the most hidden form of join. In this case a post or pin of wire is soldered onto the metal where the natural object is to be attached. The natural object has a hole drilled part-way into it that corresponds in size to the post. Adhesive is applied to the post and the natural object is fixed on. This form of cold connection is an invisible joining process and means that the natural object often appears as if it floats or sits upon the metal.

SEWING

Sewing and other textile techniques can be effective methods of bonding natural elements together. Movement, texture and colour can also be introduced when including processes such as binding, weaving, knitting, crocheting and braiding.

Dual wooden-form neckpiece, Hayley Marden, 2007. Laminated, dyed wood and gold leaf, 51 cm (20 in.) long. Photograph by John K. MacGregor.

11. Other Applications

CASTING

Casting is the process of pouring molten metal into a mould. The mould is made by using a master or by carving or pressing out a shape directly into a soft heat-resistant substance. The molten metal solidifies into the shape of the mould as it cools. This process can be used to create one-off pieces or for repeat production depending on your chosen casting method. Natural materials can be incorporated into all of the following casting processes.

Cuttlefish-casting

Cuttlefish-casting is a quick and fairly accurate casting method. Its applications are limited only by the thickness and overall dimensions of the shell. It is difficult to achieve fine details on the surface of the casting, but this is offset by the richly complex texture that is a natural by-product of this casting method.

The backplate or cuttlebone of the ordinary squid serves as the mould material. The elliptical shell is a bright-white porous material that can be easily indented by pressing a model into it. One side of this material is covered with a thin, hard crust that resembles plastic. Cuttlefish bones for casting can be purchased through jewellery suppliers and pet stores, where they are sold for use in birdcages. Sometimes you can find them washed up on the beach.

The model must be made of something solid enough to withstand being firmly pressed into the cuttlebone. Plastic or metal models are ideal. Wood or hard-wax models will work if they don't have delicate sections. It is critical that the model has no undercuts so that it can be lifted out cleanly after being pressed into the cuttlebone.

Charcoal-block casting

Simple castings can be made by using soldering blocks of natural willow charcoal. Charcoal reduces the amount of oxygen absorbed by the molten metal and thus is a particularly suitable material for casting. In this process, the shape to be cast and the crucible from which the molten metal will be poured are carved into one block of charcoal. The mould can only be used

Buds and Loom neckpiece, Beth Legg, 2005. Silver and cotton, approx. 60 cm (23⅔ in.) long. Photograph by Beth Legg.

Cut pebble mould with ring cast inside, Maike Barteldres. Silver and stone. Photograph by Jason Ingram.

once, as the charcoal degrades during removal of the casting from the block. The resulting cast will be flat on one side.

Centrifugal casting

This casting process relies on the model being burnt away, leaving an impression behind in plaster. It is most commonly used for lost-wax casting. Wax is not the only material that serves this purpose, however, and some natural objects can also be effective. Objects that burn away leaving minimum dust and deposits – such as twigs or pods – work well, but shell does not. Fine objects such as leaves can be made more robust by spraying them with hairspray, or if very delicate they can be coated with wax on one side. This does mean, however, that the texture will only be evident on one side. The burning-out of natural materials takes slightly longer and produces more fumes than the wax-model process. A centrifugal machine is a very specialist and expensive piece of equipment and means that this method of casting may have to be outsourced to a professional company or college.

ELECTROFORMING AND ELECTROPLATING

Electroplating is the process of using electrical current to coat an electrically conductive object with a relatively thin layer of metal. In essence, a skin of metal is built up into a rigid structure. Electroforming is a similar process but differs from electroplating because the skin is much thicker and can exist as a self-supporting structure if the original matrix is removed. The object being electroformed can either be a permanent part of the end product, or it can be temporary (as in the case of wax), to be removed later, leaving only the metal form – the 'electroform'. Any surface will work that is conductive and can stand up to the acids in electrolyte solution. Organic and porous materials, such as a leaf or wood, need to be sealed with several coats of varnish and conductive paint before plating. These are highly specialised processes that require specific equipment such as tanks and chemicals, but they can also be outsourced to plating companies.

ROLL-PRINTING

This is a texturing process using rolling mills, completed before any forming, shaping or piercing-out has taken place. Feathers, leaves, hair and

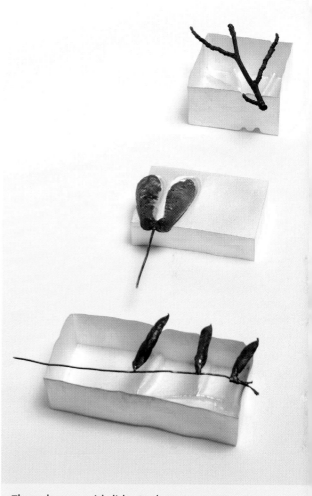

Three boxes with lids, Beth Legg, 2005.
Silver, 7–10 cm (2³/₄ x 4 in.) long.
Photograph by Beth Legg.

grasses give particularly distinct and interesting imprints. To roll-print it is best to use annealed sheet of between 0.4 mm and 0.8 mm (³/₁₆ and ³/₈ in.) thickness. After annealing and pickling, always dry the sheet well to avoid rusting the rolling mills. There has to be a certain amount of pressure in order to emboss onto the metal surface so you might want to tighten or loosen the rollers until you have found the ideal level of pressure.

PYROGRAPHY

Pyrography means 'writing with fire', and is the traditional art of using a heated tip or wire to burn or scorch designs onto natural materials such as wood or leather. Burning can be done by means of a modern solid-point tool (similar to a soldering iron) or hot-wire tool, or by a more basic method using a metal implement heated in a fire, or even sunlight concentrated with a magnifying lens.

This allows a great range of natural tones and shades to be achieved – beautiful, subtle effects can create a picture in sepia tones, or strong dark strokes can make a bold, dramatic design. Varying the type of tip used, the temperature, or the way the iron is applied to the material all create different effects. Solid-point machines offer a variety of tip shapes, and can also be used for 'branding' the wood or leather. Wire-point machines allow the artist to shape the wire into a variety of configurations, to achieve broad marks or fine lines. This work is time-consuming, done entirely by hand, with each line of a complex design individually drawn. After the design is burned in, wooden objects are often coloured, sometimes boldly, sometimes more delicately.

Light-coloured hardwoods such as sycamore, beech and birch are those most commonly used in this method, as their fine grain is not obtrusive, and they also produce the most pleasing contrast. However, other woods, such as pine or oak, are also used when required. Pyrography is also applied to leather items, using the same hot-iron technique. Leather lends itself to bold designs, and also allows very subtle shading to be achieved. Specialist vegetable-tanned leather must be used for pyrography (modern tanning methods leave chemicals in the leather which are toxic when burned), typically in light colours for good contrast.

12. Contemporary Artists' Gallery

An Alleweireldt

Radish necklace, An Alleweireldt, 2006. Radishes. Approx. 20 cm (8 in.).
Photograph by EMS photo.

An Alleweireldt believes that every single piece of material and each object around us possesses a unique beauty. To her, the shapes, materials and uses of daily objects are an inexhaustible source of inspiration for new pieces. Because 'precious' is traditionally equated to 'rare', we tend to underestimate the beauty of outwardly humble or common objects and materials. The possibilities or limitations of various materials for her do more to make them seem exciting and valuable than the question of whether or not they are rare.

Alleweireldt's work enables us to explore and discover the object and the material it is made of, and to question our perception of the outside world.

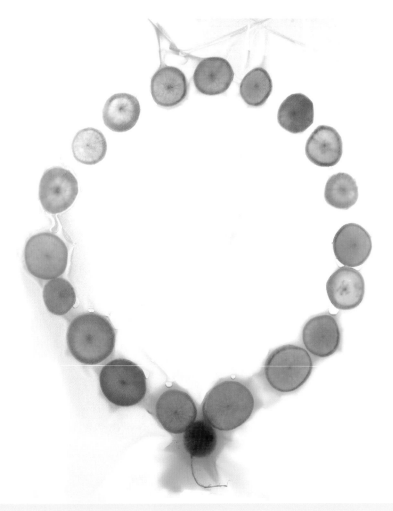

Radish necklace, An Alleweireldt, 2006. Preserved radishes, plastic bag, vacuum-formed. Approx. 20 cm (8 in.). Photograph by EMS photo.

She chose to work with the radish as her material because in her view 'the radish is probably one of the most humble but also most beautiful of all vegetables. It would seem disrespectful to try and reproduce its prettiness in an object.'

Born in 1974 in Ostend, Belgium, Alleweireldt studied at the Academy of Fine & Applied Arts in Antwerp, and then at The Royal College of Art, London. She lives and works in Belgium.

KIRSTEN BAK

Born in Aalborg, Denmark, Bak believes that 'we focus a lot on the shell and seldom look underneath. The details capture us and prevent us from looking further on.'

These rings made of wood and plastic take their form from tree boughs. Nature dictates the form and the lines of the wood create the ornamentation of the ring – each ring being unique. Bak gathers forks of plane trees, selecting sections where the branch divides into two or more. The sections are hollowed out, leaving behind a thin and fragile residual surface used to create the ring. Bak allows nature to shape her forms, with the wood patterns and markings forming the decorative facet of the piece, while a layer of stabilising plastic sheaths the exterior.

These pieces challenge our preconceived ideas about the environment and lead us to understand that we are living in a plastic world. Bak won the Inhorgenta Innovation Prize in 2006 for this series of work.

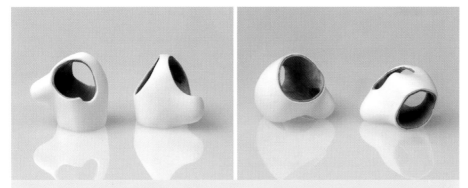

Unicated rings, Kirsten Bak, 2005. Plane wood, plastic coating. 2.5 x 2.5 x 3.5 cm (1 x 1 x 1½ in.). Photographs by Kirsten Bak.

Necklace, Ela Bauer, 2005. Latex and copper gauze, 45 cm (18 in.). Photograph by Ela Bauer.

ELA BAUER

Born in 1960 in Warsaw, Poland, Ela Bauer studied at the Rietveld Academie in Holland, during which she endeavoured to investigate the roots of what makes something a 'jewel'. Through this exploration her jewels became more like objects. They developed into statements about terms such as 'preciousness', 'wearability' and 'decoration'. The silicone rubber that she uses is a perfect medium to create the kind of forms that fascinate her and to express the atmosphere of what she calls 'liquid definitions'. The silicone is a morph, enabling her to create 'sharp', cast elements and structures, as well as 'flowing' surfaces.

The organic, cell- and treelike forms in her work express a preoccupation with the fact that everything – situations, definitions and people – is in continuous movement and constant change. Bauer believes that 'the processes of change in the organisms – growth, development, and disintegration – are the ultimate metaphors for this phenomenon. They have a great influence on my "organic form-vocabulary".'

Bauer has recently made works constructed of cast-silicone 'cells'. Those cells are often connected by means of sewing – a joining technique which symbolises protection, mending and reconstruction. There is a certain contradiction between the modern aesthetic implied in the use of silicone and the technique of sewing; nevertheless, the two fit perfectly together, strengthening each other's impact.

Bauer's sewing was purely functional to begin with, but very quickly she began to 'draw' with the needle and the thread on the surface of the rubber, creating veins, rivers, paths and scars. Colour is very important to Bauer. It

Necklace, Ela Bauer, 2005. Latex and raw coral, 44 cm (17½ in.), photograph by Ela Bauer.

determines to a great extent the meanings and atmosphere of the work. She usually mixes pigments into the silicone, and then paints her pieces into three dimensions layer upon layer. This manner of working enables her to control the colour, thickness and transparency of the work.

Ela Bauer has exhibited in Schmuck, and her work is included in the Dänner Collection in the Pinakothek der Moderne, Munich.

SEBASTIAN BUESCHER

These pieces are from Buescher's recent collection of work entitled Imperfection Please. The work is strongly process-based, and inspired by ritualistic jewellery and ancient relics. Buescher's jewels have become small communicators of a common contemporary motto: 'Life is too short'. The materials themselves address this theme, as the fragile earthenware used could also be seen as a metaphor for the fragility of both body and soul. Buescher takes the jewel out of the purely decorative realm and places it into one in which a piece can no longer be worn without awareness of a deeper meaning. Buescher's lesson is not to give up when we break, but to pick ourselves up and move beyond it, which he believes can most easily be achieved when we take our mind off the goal itself and immerse ourselves in the process.

According to Buescher himself, 'Sometimes the material, or object, is complete and I have to do nothing more than use it as it is. Other instances make me dissect the object, looking for something I haven't seen or something that feels meaningful. A lot of these objects are about history, in other words time and experience. Things from the river have been tumbled and washed for maybe a thousand years, trees have grown over centuries and second-hand materials have been used, perhaps stolen, lost or given away. This formula is then applied to my ideas and somehow comes together as a piece.'

Born in 1978 in Cologne, Germany, Buescher is currently studying for an MA in Fine Art at the University of Brighton and has just completed work on solo shows for Galerie Rob Koudijs, Amsterdam, and Alternatives Gallery, Rome.

The Widow Maker, Sebastian Buescher, 2007. Glass, black-widow spider egg cases, poison. 12 x 6 x 3 cm (4¾ x 2⅓ x 1⅓ in.). Photograph by Sebastian Buescher.

Blood Sweat Tears, Sebastian Buescher, 2007. Earthenware, blood, sweat, tears, wool, garnet, steel. 55 cm (21⅔ in.). Photograph by Sebastian Buescher.

ORNELLA IANNUZZI

Ornella Iannuzzi was born in 1983 in Chambéry, France and recently undertook the MA in Goldsmithing, Silversmithing, Metalwork & Jewellery at the Royal College of Art, London. Iannuzzi is interested in the process of 'creation' in the biggest sense of the word – the genesis of things. Her work is concerned with the basic elements of the vegetable and mineral worlds, the origins of these materials being a great source of inspiration for her. 'From these materials, I would like to give the feeling that nature itself gave birth to

ABOVE Ring *Look after me no.1*, Ornella Iannuzzi, 2007. Painted copper, quartz crystal, moss & cactus plant (Haworthia attenuata), 8 x 6.5 x 10 cm (3¼ x 2½ x 4 in.). Photograph by Amanda Mansell.

BELOW Ring *Look after me no.2*, Ornella Iannuzzi, 2007. Silver, carborundum, moss & cactus plant (*Escobaria Sneedii ssp.leei*), 6 x 6.5 x 9.5 cm (2¼ x 2½ x 3¾ in.). Photograph by Dominic Sweeny.

my jewels and that they actually grow on the body. All my creations are one-of-a-kind.'

There is a definite feeling of random germination and natural balance about her work. It suggests the quirky determination of nature – the weed that grows through the tarmac.

IRIS EICHENBERG

Neckpiece, Iris Eichenberg, 2004. Porcelain, cotton, lead, leather, 40 cm (16 in.). Photograph by Francis Willemstijn.

Iris Eichenberg is known for her highly personal and sensual language in which the vulnerability of the human body is a constant theme. Eichenberg's hybrid creations are hard to categorise; the forms are compelling, referring to the intricate systems of living organisms. Many of her small objects, and also larger works such as pieces of furniture and installations, are ambiguous: mysterious and sexual, but also familiar and personal.

In her own words, Eichenberg creates 'a microcosmic view of nature's forms, the shapes could be renditions of delicate wild flowers but are equally reminiscent of parts of an animal or human body such as fingers, teats or orifices'.

The materials the artist employs are often distinctly opposite: warm wool with cold silver or soft pink wax with a sliver of hard pear wood, a symbiotic combination which creates a precise and delicate balance within each piece. Eichenberg favours materials that retain the traces of their process and hence have a living presence. She enjoys working with wool, as its textures evoke primal warmth and have an instantly appealing tactility. For Eichenberg, knitting is a natural choice of material and method, as its structure can be totally spontaneous and involves a process

Neckpiece, Iris Eichenberg, 2004.
Silver, wool, 60 cm (24 in.).
Photograph by Ron Zijlstra.

which is 'about the speed of making things grow. You can change the form easily, and it is a way of letting things grow without a definitive end.' The fragility of the human body is a theme that is consistently brought up in her pieces. Her work is both plant and animal – twigs and fingers, tubers and umbilical chords – evoking birth and growth.

Iris Eichenberg was born in Göttingen, Germany in 1965. After training as a nurse she went on to study at the Gerrit Rietveld Academie in the Netherlands, where she was the Head of the Jewellery Department from 2000 to 2007. She is the recipient of prestigious awards including the Gerrit Rietveld Academie Award, the H. Hofmann Prize and the Artist Stimulation Award, which have all helped to establish her status as a leader in the field of art jewellery. Recent solo exhibitions include one at the Galerie Louise Smit, Amsterdam, and her work is also included in numerous private collections and permanent public collections including the Stedelijk Museum, Amsterdam, the Gemeente Museum, Arnhem, the Textielmuseum, Tilburg, all in the Netherlands, and the Schmuck Museum, Pforzheim, Germany.

KATY HACKNEY

Katy Hackney was born in Dundee and studied at Edinburgh College of Art and the Royal College of Art. She uses an unorthodox range of materials, such as vintage Formica, cellulose acetate and plywood, to create unique jewellery that displays a charming and quirky lack of compromise. Hackney's work appears delightfully uncomplicated but in truth it involves intricate and challenging processes requiring skill and expertise.

Hackney's work is held in the Crafts Council Collection, London, the Royal Museum of Scotland, Edinburgh, and the Montreal Museum of Decorative Arts in Canada.

Ring, Katy Hackney, 2006. Formica, wood, silver, 2.5 x 3.5 x 5 cm (1 x 1³/₈ x 2 in.). Photograph by Sussie Ahlberg.

White brooch with twig, Katy Hackney, 2006. Formica, wood, bamboo, cellulose acetate, silver, steel, 5 x 4 x 2 cm (2 x 1¹/₂ x ³/₄ in.). Photograph by Sussie Ahlberg.

PIRITTA HOUTTU

Born in Helsinki, Finland in 1983, Piritta Houttu is a young maker from the jewellery and stoneware design course at Lappeenranta. Houttu's work is constructed by attaching small, almost identical elements to each other in different ways. She likens the process to the way in which a house can be built from many bricks.

In this work it is evident that even fragile materials, like very thinly cut stone, become durable and resilient when many pieces are layered upon one another.

LEFT *Mustakeltainen* brooch, Piritta Houttu, 2007. Granite, epoxy, yellow pigment, silver, 7 x 5 cm (2³/₄ x 2 in.). Photograph by Piritta Houttu.

RIGHT *Vihreä* brooch, Piritta Houttu, 2007. Granite aventurin, epoxy, blue pigment, silver, 7 x 7 cm (2³/₄ x 2³/₄ in.). Photograph by Piritta Houttu.

Hsiu-Hsuan Huan

The artist Eva Hesse said of her work, 'I do not believe art can be based on an idea of composition or form. In fact, my idea is to counteract everything I've ever learned or been taught about those things, to find something else, so it is inevitable that it is my life, my feeling, my thoughts...' Hsiu-Hsuan Huan is driven to make jewellery by a similar creative ethos.

He begins by exploring the qualities of the materials that he selects for his works, such as felt, silk and hair. All of these materials hold special meanings for him. Huan approaches his jewellery-making from a painting perspective. He explores the conceptual connection between two-dimensional painting and three-dimensional objects. As a result, process is very important to him.

'To me, painting is deep. What the audience sees in the work conjures up what the artist might have felt when he or she put every stroke carefully onto the canvas. The creative process transmutes the painter's time and thoughts into a picture. I am interested in the transition from painting to craft-making. In that, my thinking process is authentically reflected in my craft.'

Hsiu-Hsuan Huan studied at the Birmingham Institute of Art and Design (BIAD).

TOP *Sketch 3* neckpiece, Hsiu-Hsuan Huan, 2006. Silk, 45 cm x 20 cm (17³/₄ x 8 in.). Photograph by Hsiu-Hsuan Huan.

BELOW *Tracing Memory 1*, Hsiu-Hsuan Huan, 2006. Charcoal, silk sheet, ink, linen, dye, 48 cm x 16 cm (19 x 6¹/₄ in.). Photograph by Hsiu-Hsuan Huan.

METTE T. JENSEN

Mette Jensen works with a mixture of precious and non-precious materials, exploiting the special characteristics of each one. Her inspiration in some cases is the material itself or the way it is normally used; in others it comes from sculptures, architecture, mathematics or other areas where interesting forms ask to be translated into jewellery.

In Jensen's main collection the materials used are wood and silver; both being curved to achieve the desired forms which in this are

ABOVE *Bracelet no. 6214*, Mette T. Jensen, 2005 & 2006. Beech and silver, approx. 9.5 x 9.5 x 9.5 cm (3³/₄ x 3³/₄ x 3³/₄ in.) each. Photograph by Joël Degen.

BELOW *Bracelets no. 529* and *6216*, Mette T. Jensen, 2006. Beech and silver, approx. 9.5 x 9.5 x 2.5 cm (3³/₄ x 3³/₄ x 1 in.). Photograph by Joël Degen.

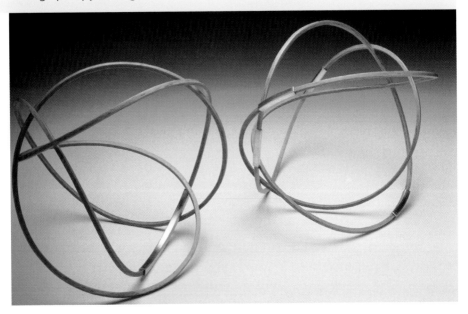

inspired by furniture and ships. The flexibility and lightness of the wood makes it possible to create reasonably large pieces as well as unusual fittings and forms that challenge the imagination.

BETH LEGG

I was born in 1981 in Caithness in Scotland. The county sits at the very top of the British mainland and is called 'the lowlands beyond the Highlands' because of its flat moors and huge skies. It is a bleak and fragile landscape.

The remote environment I come from has strongly influenced the work I produce. I am fascinated by the way in which the natural elements sculpt the vast open spaces in the far north of Scotland, and I aim for this to be reflected in my work. My pieces explore ideas surrounding the embedded

Caged Bird necklace, Beth Legg, 2006. Bird bone, oxidised silver, 150 cm (59 in.). Photograph by Beth Legg.

Caged Bird brooch, Beth Legg, 2006. Bird bone, oxidised silver, steel, 4.5 x 7 cm (1³/₄ x 2³/₄ in.). Photograph by Beth Legg.

object and memory. The found objects I use are metaphors for recovered memory. I see these materials as artefacts which have a powerful relationship with the environment I have taken them from. I tend to work instinctively with my materials rather than contriving designs beforehand. Drawing and photography also play an important part in my research process, allowing me to record both the developments at the bench and exterior influences drawn from different landscapes. I enjoy the labour of hand-tool processes, and I find the approach of designing through making both intellectually and emotionally rewarding. When they are not being worn I would like my pieces to take on the character of still lives through the contrasts I seek to evoke in each assemblage. I aim for my work to be seen as a moving dialogue, each piece an exploration of component elements encompassing themes of honesty, landscape and memory.

ANNA LEWIS

A feather is said to be the measure of your soul. Anna Lewis uses feathers with a very delicate, ghostlike quality to create body pieces which wrap around and embrace the neck and shoulders like a security blanket, evoking feelings of protection and memory. Lewis says of her work; 'The sensitivity and the lightness of the feather is juxtaposed with the idea of memory being heavy with meaning, commenting on the ambiguous nature of memory as it fades into a mythical vision. Some feathers have been printed with traces of memory and are either layered or stand alone.'

Trace, Anna Lewis, 2006. Layered feather necklace, feathers, millinery wire, crin, 30 to 40 cm (12 x 16 in.) long. Photograph by Anna Lewis.

Trace, Anna Lewis, 2006. Layered feather necklace, feathers, millinery wire, crin, 30 to 40 cm (12 x 16 in.) long. Photograph by Anna Lewis.

Since graduating from Middlesex University in 2000, memories of past lives and objects have been an influence on Lewis's work, as well as an appreciation of all that has been constructed or touched by hand. Her layered feather necklaces are assembled using millinery wire and are layered with hand-cut white goose feathers, some of which are hand-printed with colours and images.

JULIE MOLLENHAUER

Julie Mollenhauer has been drawn to working with natural materials since she began making jewellery. She puts this down to the soft qualities of materials such as amber, which has a plasticity and workability that lends itself well to hand-tool processes. Amber continually reminds us of its past as part of a living organism. Mollenhauer is attracted in particular to its lightness and warmth.

Julie Mollenhauer was born in 1960 in Kassel, Germany. She undertook a goldsmith apprenticeship in Göttingen, Germany and then went on to study at the Gerrit Rietveld Academie in Amsterdam. She shows her work with Galerie Marzee in Nijmegen in the Netherlands.

Necklace, Julie Mollenhauer, 2006. Amber, gold. 18 x 18 x 1.5 cm
(7 x 7 x ⅔ in.). Photograph by Thomas Lenden.

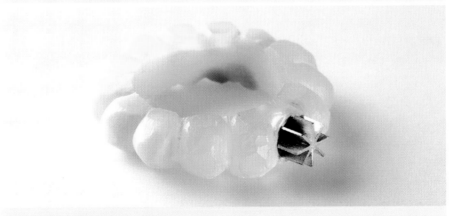

Ring, Julie Mollenhauer, 2006. Amber, gold. 2.7 x 3 x 0.5 cm (1 x 1⅕ x ⅕ in.).
Photograph by Thomas Lenden.

EVERT NIJLAND

Evert Nijland was born in 1971 in Oldenzaal in the Netherlands. He studied, and now teaches, at the Gerrit Rietveld Academie in Amsterdam. For the body of work entitled *Venezia*, Nijland has taken the bead as a starting point. After a visit to Venice he was struck by the atmosphere of the city as a whole, which was always closely connected to the sound, rhythm and movement of the omnipresent water.

The simple principle of a bead allows him to make large necklaces consisting of different stringed parts. He has gone beyond the limitations of the traditional beaded necklace by increasing the size of the beads, and by making each bead unique. The accomplished craftsmanship of his work is something to admire in itself. There is a clear appearance of power and depth to the wood once he has finished working it, a strong and beautiful presence akin to a piece of antique furniture. Nijland is conscious of the long tradition in jewellery of searching for the meaning of beauty, which his work reinterprets in a context that is wholly contemporary.

Nijland's work can be seen in the Schmuck Museum, Pforzheim, in Germany and the Stedelijk Museum in Amsterdam.

Stucco necklace, from the series *Venezia*, Evert Nijland, 2006. Mahogany, silver, porcelain, 70 cm (27½ in.) long. Photograph by Eddo Hartmann.

Profile Argento necklace, from the series *Venezia*, Evert Nijland, 2006. Ebony, silver, textile, 60 cm (24 in.) long. Photograph by Eddo Hartmann.

NATALYA PINCHUK

In her *Growth* series of work, Natalya Pinchuk combines wool, plastic flower parts and enamelled copper forms into miniature landscape systems. The wearing of these simulated growths can be thought of as an ironic act of assimilation: the artificial becoming absorbed into the landscape of the

Growth series brooch, Natalya Pinchuk, 2006. 15 x 12 x 8 cm (6 x 4¾ x 3 in.). Wool, copper, enamel, plastic, thread. Photograph by Natalya Pinchuk.

Growth series brooch, Natalya Pinchuk, 2006. Wool, copper, enamel, plastic, thread. 5.5 x 11 x 5 cm (2⅛ x 4⅓ x 2 in.). Photograph by Natalya Pinchuk.

body. This act of incorporation hints at the growing intrusion of the artificial within our surroundings.

Growth brooches and necklaces are attractive, fun, wearable pieces with colourful surfaces and amusing plastic vegetation growing out of them. The same jewellery pieces, however, can also suggest unease by alluding to the unseen, un-familiar and menacing growths that lurk within the body and the environment.

Combining wool with enamelled surfaces and plastic heightens the ambiguity over what is natural and what artificial: while these pieces allude to nature and its potential colours and forms, they do not correspond to anything specific. Instead of a scientific exploration of actual changes in the body, Pinchuk is more interested in the perceived, imagined and feared interpretations of the changes inside or around us.

Natalya Pinchuk often employs a combination of freshly felted wool and recycled clothing. In the context of clothing, the clean spun wool threads are knitted together, connoting warmth and protection. Raw or matted-together wool evokes a more primal existence, accentuating the animal parts of our character that fashion and consumerism try to hide away. Pinchuk is aiming to expose the body through the socially acceptable form of adornment.

Natalya Pinchuk is the Assistant Professor of the Art Metal Jewellery Program at Austin State University, Nacogdoches. She has exhibited her work with Charon Kransen Arts at SOFA Chicago and SOFA New York, and Mobilia Gallery in Cambridge, Massachusetts.

LAURA SAARNIA

Working primarily in raw crystal, Saarnia's pieces incorporate photographs from old family albums and speak of buried memories and fading nostalgia. The transparency and luminosity of quartz are the qualities that draw her to work with this stone. Saarnia's work possesses a wistful melancholy and is haunting in its depiction of the loss of clarity.

Born in 1984 in Lappeenranta, Finland, Saarnia recently graduated from the Jewellery and Stonework Design course at the South Karelian Polytechnic in her home town.

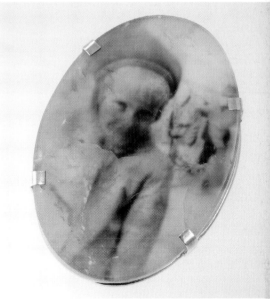

TOP Brooch, Laura Saarnia, 2007. Quartz, silver, Lazertran, 6 x 4 cm (2¹/₄ x 1¹/₂ in.). Photograph by Kimmo Heikkilä.

RIGHT Brooch, Laura Saarnia, 2007. Quartz, silver, Lazertran, 6 x 4cm (2¹/₄ x 1¹/₂ in.). Photograph by Kimmo Heikkilä.

Lucy Sarneel

Nature is an important point of reference to Lucy Sarneel. The relative naturalness or artificiality of an object fascinates her and results in the creation of forms reminiscent of flowers, plants or twigs. She says, 'One assimilates power from a jewel by wearing it and at the same time one adds power and meaning to it; this imaginary 'breathing in and out' of a jewel fascinates me. To me a jewel represents a place in the world in which one can lose oneself like in the sparkling of a diamond or the careful observation of little plants or moss.'

Ideas about time play an important role in her work – personal history, historic time and universal time. She challenges herself to maintain a tension between the restricted material space and the unlimited mental and spiritual space of a jewel. Her craftsmanship transforms everyday materials into precious objects.

Lucy Sarneel was born in 1961 in Maastricht, the Netherlands. She studied at the Gerrit Rietveld Academie, Amsterdam from1985 to1989, and has gone on to have solo shows at Galerie Marzee at Nijmegen in the Netherlands, Galerie HNOSS at Gothenburg in Sweden, Tactile in Geneva, and Charon Kransen Arts at SOFA Chicago. Sarneel's work is held in several public collections including the Montreal Museum of Decorative Arts, The Marzee Collection at Nijmegen, the Museum voor Moderne Kunst at Arnhem, and the Stedelijk Museum in Amsterdam.

Untitled brooch, Lucy Sarneel, 2006. 11 x 15 x 3 cm (4⅓ x 6 x 1⅕ in.). Wooden knob, antique textile, silver. Photograph by Eric Knoote.

Zeebauw necklace, Lucy Sarneel, 2003. Antique textile, thread, silver, shells filled with epoxy, zinc. 35 x 18.5 x 2 cm (13¾ x 7¼ x ¾ in.). Photograph by Ron Zijlstra.

CONSTANZE SCHREIBER

Nearly all of Constanze Schreiber's works are inspired by antique jewellery pieces – predominantly those of the 19th and early 20th centuries. These pieces often have symbolic meanings and possess a powerful beauty. She is drawn to them because of their function as protective amulets or memento-mori pieces. Schreiber aims in her work to express the essential themes of love, life and death, reinterpreting the forms and symbols of the past in a contemporary context.

In her series of pieces entitled Ornament and Crime, Schreiber has created necklaces and brooches filled with lead balls. These pieces sit around your neck or on your chest with the weight of an animal – heavy and soft;

Eugenie brooch, Constanze Schreiber, 2004. Fur, lead, silver, 12 x 8.5 cm (4³/₄ x 3³/₈ in.). Photograph by Edo Kuipers.

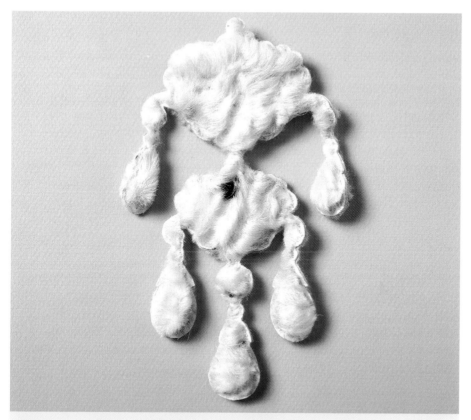

Constanze Schreiber, *Marie* brooch, 2005. Fur, lead, silver, 14cm x 8cm x 2cm (5½ x 3⅛ x ¾ in.). Photograph by Edo Kuipers.

cumbersome and comforting. She is drawing attention to the relationship between mankind and nature. 'We use nature as raw material, as matter to which we give form. Are we conscious of this when we get our ready-prepared and packed products out of the shop? We live off nature; that is essential. With my work I hope to make people realise the value and the origins of natural materials.'

Schreiber wants us to treat natural materials with respect and be conscious of their sources. This jewellery reminds us of the renewing qualities of nature and the soothing qualities that both nature and adornment have in common.

Constanze Schreiber was born in 1977 in Siegen, Germany. After studying at both the Goldsmithing School in Pforzheim, Germany and the Gerrit Rietveld Academie in Amsterdam, she has gone on to exhibit at Gallery Ra, Amsterdam and Gallery Ornamentum, New York.

JOE SHEEHAN

There has always been a shifting between the categories of sculpture and jewellery in Joe Sheehan's practice, and this is a direct reflection of the manner in which the carving culture of the Pacific has developed.

Sheehan was born in Nelson, New Zealand in 1976, and follows in his father's footsteps as a jade-worker. After some time carving in a commercial workshop for his father, Sheehan began to make his own work influenced by the experience of working within this tourist-trade environment. Moved by the way that commercial success had stunted the creative growth of the carving culture in New Zealand, he began to focus on how spirituality had degenerated into superstition, and the way objects and ornaments made in an era of modern machinery still looked like they were the products of a Stone Age culture.

The validity of both material and object is highly important to Sheehan. Through working jade he has exposed its potential as a medium for relevant contemporary art practice. In his recent work he has carved versions of everyday objects – a set of keys, a tape, a series of Bic pens, batteries, etc. – modern artefacts that speak of shared experiences and today's blurred cultural contexts.

Sheehan says of his practice, 'In my work I am trying to make objects that spark some tactile memory in the viewer/handler so that a re-evaluation of what that thing is and what it means takes place.' Through his skilful handling of hard stone we are forced to address the way jade's cultural associations are promoted while also contemplating thoughtful commentaries on the way we see everyday objects.

Russian Dolls, Joe Sheehan, 2005. Tiki, Russian jade, 4.5 to 13 cm (1³/₄ x 5¹/₈ in.). Photograph by Nick Barr.

BETTINA SPECKNER

Bettina Speckner makes jewellery of fragmented stories about recollection and beauty. She combines natural materials like shells, coral and minerals with each other or with photographic images in a sensitive and refined manner. The images range widely – nature, landscape, architecture, or still lives – etched in zinc or burned in enamel, monochrome and inert, like a moment from a dream. By adding abstract forms and unusual materials, Speckner integrates ferrotypes – portrait photographs from the second half of the 19th century – into intriguing, intimate and quirky collages.

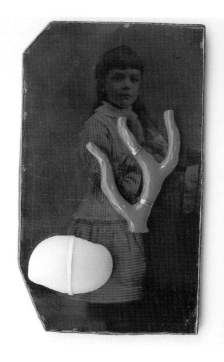

Brooch, Bettina Speckner, 2004. Ferrotype, silver, coral, snail, 9.5 x 7.5 cm (3³/₄ x 3 in.). Photograph by Bettina Speckner.

Brooch, Bettina Speckner, 2007. Enamel photograph, silver, shell, 7 x 7.5 cm (2³/₄ x 3 in.). Photograph by Bettina Speckner.

Speckner creates a visual poetry that carries you into timeless and nostalgic worlds. Her making process consists of a series of trial constructions and interventions that unite into beautifully balanced compositions. The work is distinguished by unique compositions of material, form and image that feel both formally correct and unexpectedly enlightening.

'I never work with the intention to decorate things or to make them look prettier,' Speckner points out. 'I try to discover the soul of an object or the essence of a photograph and want to shape something new which appeals to me and to other people far beyond the optical appearance.' Speckner works from 'collections' of representations, materials and objects to establish fresh affiliations between them. This inevitably results in divergent layers of form and visual information. In some pieces the material becomes image, and vice versa. The strangeness of the natural form of coral within a familiar frame could suggest organs and bone. The stories her jewellery tells are about beautiful memories, the pleasure of collecting and little moments of happiness.

Bettina Speckner was born in 1962 in Offenburg, Germany and went on to study under Prof. Herman Jünger and Prof. Otto Künzli. Her work is held in various collections including the Danner Foundation, Munich, the Schmuck Museum, Pforzheim and the Royal College of Art Collection, London.

TERHI TOLVANEN

Terhi Tolvanen's work is about human intervention in nature. She believes that, because nature keeps on growing, this interference needs to be maintained and continued. This interaction between the two has become the central theme of her jewellery. In her choice of materials she is also seeking to highlight the borders between the natural and the artificial.

Birch & Chain necklace, Terhi Tolvanen, 2007. Wood, silver, steel, smoky quartz, paint, 17 cm (6³/₄ in.) diameter. Photograph by Francis Willemstijn.

Swingy necklace, Terhi Tolvanen, 2007. Hazelnut wood, smoky quartz, silver, 18 cm (7 in.) diameter. Photograph by Francis Willemstijn.

Tolvanen likens her pieces to plants. Partly from nature, partly manmade, they show the symbiosis between nature and humanity. No matter how eagerly we plant, nurture and cut away excess growth, the grass between the paving stones is certain to emerge again. Tolvanen often combines delicate materials such as silk, silver thread and porcelain with dense, earthy materials such as wood and minerals, both rare and easily accessible. These materials seem to have sprung from a place that is spiritual and enchanted, forming a unique sculptural symbiotic relationship.

Terhi Tolvanen was born in 1968 in Helsinki, Finland and studied at The Gerrit Rietveld Academie in Amsterdam. She exhibits with Galerie Louise Smit in Amsterdam.

TARJA TUUPANEN

'The main material in my work is stone, which I love for its versatility and challenging nature, and hate for its trickiness and limitations.' Tuupanen carves her stone thinly, sometimes to its edge, looking for boundaries and interesting sides of the material. She works this unyielding material in such a way that it begins to speak of a sensuality and softness. The forms in her jewellery are often reminiscent of the human body. Lips, rims, edges and openings appear to us and take on a further context when worn – the cold material absorbing the body's heat. Tuupanen is concerned with subtle questions of gender: how the genders differ from each other and how they are also in many ways the same.

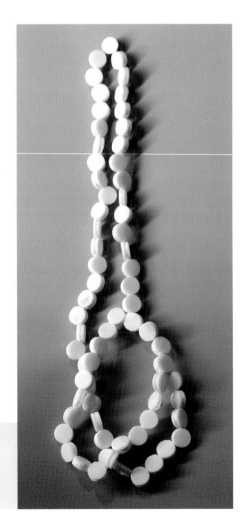

Brooch, Tarja Tuupanen, 2006. Marble, silver, pearl silk, 22 x 5 x 1 cm (8³⁄₄ x 2 x ¹⁄₄ in.). Photograph by Kimmo Heikkilä.

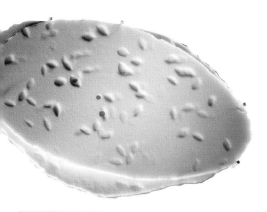

Brooch, Tarja Tuupanen, 2006. White quartz, silver, 7 x 5 x 0.5 cm (2³/₄ x 2 x ¹/₂ in.). Photograph by Jaan Seitsara.

Born in 1973 in Lieksa, Finland, Tuupanen went on to study at the Department of Jewellery and Stonework at the South Karelia Polytechnic in Lappeenranta, Finland. Since 2000 she has been a teacher of stonework within the specialised programme of jewellery art at this school. Her work is in the collections of the Rhöska Museet in Gothenburg, Sweden, The Françoise van den Bosch Foundation in the Netherlands, and the Regional Museum at Turnov in the Czech Republic.

JACOMIJN VAN DER DONK

The work of Jacomijn van der Donk always has a vivid and sensual relationship with nature. Born in the Netherlands in 1963, she went on to study in the Gerrit Rietveld Academie, Amsterdam, and in the 16 years since graduating has developed an enviable body of work. The starting point of her most recent work is branches – simple but rigid shapes which she uses directly as a base material for her pieces. She works them so that they are indistinguishable from coral or bones. From this foundation material flexible shapes develop resembling

Bracelet, Jacomijn van der Donk, 2006. Goat hair, silver, 35 cm (13³/₄ in.) long. Photograph by Ole Eshuis.

Necklace, Jacomijn van der Donk, 2006. Beech twig, epoxy, copper, goat hair, 113 cm (44½ in.) long. Photograph by Ole Eshuis.

drawings in the air. Her work speaks of blood and nerve systems moving through polished bones, or blossom that has just burst out.

The use of goat hair from brushes on bracelets and neckpieces highlights the softness and sensitivity of the skin on which they are to be worn. Van der Donk wishes the movement of these pieces as they are worn to feel like a sensual caress. 'One should experience a very intimate and private feeling with my ornaments,' she says.

The independent movement of elements within each piece is characteristic of the Van der Donk's work; it allows the jewellery to adapt to the natural body shape of the wearer. She believes that the work should feel good, follow the movement of the body, and be wearable at all times. It is not the onlooker who must be seduced but the one who wears it. Therefore, the sensual beauty of the piece reveals itself fully only when worn on the body itself.

Van der Donk's work is held in the collections of The Stedelijk Museum, Amsterdam, The Fondation National d'Art Contemporain, Paris and The Royal College of Art, London.

FRANCIS WILLEMSTIJN

Francis Willemstijn is creatively driven by the unique history of the materials she chooses to work with. Her solemn and haunting pieces constitute suggestive collages of her homeland's past and traditions. Willemstijn's work is very much about being Dutch. She draws heavily on her cultural heritage for both symbol and material in her pieces, which evoke a lost world. 'I feel connected to Dutch history,' explains Willemstijn. 'I try to translate my heritage, the clay of my own country, into jewellery.

Bracelet, Francis Willemstijn, 2006. Bog oak, wood. 19 x 8 cm (7½ x 3⅛ in.). Photograph by Francis Willemstijn.

Cheesehead necklace, Francis Willemstijn, 2006. Oak, textile. 40 cm (15¾ in.) long. Photograph by Francis Willemstijn.

Willemstijn employs materials that are strongly connected with the source of her inspiration – Dutch land and history. Ebony and rosewood, viewed as luxurious materials centuries ago, feature prominently in her works. Bog oak (oak wood that has been submerged in swamps for many years) also has a very strong presence in her pieces. The fact that bog oak was once used as a substitute for jet in mourning jewellery emphasises the monumental quality and sense of loss evident in her work. Willemstijn's work is proof that a person's cultural heritage can be meaningfully renewed in our own time. The pieces forge a connection between past and present, tradition and innovation, death and life.

Francis Willemstijn was born in 1973 in Hoorn, the Netherlands and also studied jewellery there at The Gerrit Rietveld Academie. She has had two solo exhibitions at Galerie Louise Smit, Amsterdam, and her work is included in the Marzee Collection, Nijmegen.

SAYUMI YOKOUCHI

Sayumi Yokouchi's approach to work is one of endless experimentation with materials and processes. She sees her jewellery as elements that echo the growth and perpetual renewal of the urban landscape, encompassing synthetic (urban) and precious (natural) materials. Yokouchi is inspired by lichen systems that take form and grow in patches on rocks, tree trunks and soil, resembling the communities we inhabit. Living in an urban environment where the natural and artificial grow and live together, she sees this relationship as being similar to the symbiotic life of lichens and their hosts.

Copia 3, Sayumi Yokouchi, 2006. Felt, silver, nylon, dye, white gold, 5 x 5 x 1.5 cm (2 x 2 x ⁵/₈ in.). Photograph by Ralph Gabriner.

Yellow Brooch, Sayumi Yokouchi, 2006. Felt, silver, nylon, dye, 8 x 4 cm (3⅛ x 1½ in.). Photograph by Ralph Gabriner.

Yokouchi manipulates felted material, often incorporating industrial felt polishing buffs, creating clustered elements that suggest a combination of fungus and algae-like ornaments. The felt buffs come in many shapes and sizes and are sawn, cut, manipulated and shaped with tools. Intense stitching work then allows her to render this material into a more specific form and lends a more worked appearance to the finished object. The pieces are then dyed in different shades and colours, suggesting life and growth. Sayumi Yokouchi's organic forms act as miniature landscapes in jewellery, while her bright colours create a feeling of active growth, intertwining with the natural beauty of her work.

Yokouchi was born in Tokyo and now lives in New York. She received her BFA in Metal Arts at California College of Arts and Crafts and her MFA in Metal Arts at the State University of New York at New Paltz.

Galleries and Websites

Alternatives (Rome)	http://www.alternatives.it/
Annick Zufferey (Geneva)	http://www.galerie-annickzufferey.com
Antipode (Moscow)	http://www.antipode.ru
Baetrice Lang (Berne)	http://www.beatricelang.ch
Bielak (Cracow)	http://www.galeriabielak.pl
Biro (Munich)	http://www.galerie-biro.de
Charon Kransen (New York)	http://www.charonkransenarts.com
Contacto Directo (Lisbon)	http://www.contactodirecto.org
Detail (Dusseldorf)	http://www.ultra-vires.de/detail3/index.html
Deux Poissons (Tokyo)	http://www.deuxpoissons.com
Elsa Vanier (Paris)	http://www.elsa-vanier.fr
Fingers (Auckland)	http://www.fingers.co.nz
Flow (London)	http://www.flowgallery.co.uk
Friends of Charlotta (Zurich)	http://www.foc.ch
Funaki (Melbourne)	http://www.galleryfunaki.com.au
Hnoss (Gothenburg)	http://www.konstepidemin.com/hnoss
Influx (Calgary)	http://www.influxgallery.com
Ingot (Fitzroy, Victoria)	http://www.studioingot.com.au
Isogaya (Tokyo)	http://www.isogaya.co.jp
Jungblut (Luxembourg)	http://www.jungblut.lu
Katherine Kalaf (Cottesloe, W. Aus.)	http://www.katherinekalafgallery.com
Koch (Cadolzburg)	http://www.kochgalerie.de
Konsthantverkarna (Stockholm)	http://www.konsthantverkarna.se/khv
Konsthantverkscentrum (Stockholm)	http://www.konsthantverkscentrum.se
Lachaert (Tielrode)	http://www.lachaert.com
Le Arti Orafe (Florence)	http://www.leartiorafeartgallery.it
Legiokunst (Tilburg)	http://www.legiokunst.nl
Lesley Craze (London)	http://www.lesleycrazegallery.co.uk
Long strides in tiny shoes (Amsterdam)	http://www.longstridesintinyshoes.com
LouiseSmit (Amsterdam)	http://www.louisesmit.nl
Lous Martin (Delft)	http://www.delftweb.nl/pages/lousmartin/site.html
Lucca Preziosa (Lucca)	http://www.luccapreziosa.it

Marijke (Padua)	http://www.marijkestudio.com
Marzee (Nijmegen)	http://www.marzee.nl
Metal (Copenhagen)	http://www.galeriemetal.dk
Milano (Warsaw)	http://www.milano.arts.pl
Norsu (Helsinki)	http://www.norsu.info
Nutida Svenskt Silver (Stockholm)	http://www.nutida.nu
Object (Sydney)	http://www.object.com.au
Object Design (Vancouver)	http://www.objectdesigngallery.com
Oona (Berlin)	http://www.oona-galerie.de
Orefo (Cologne)	http://www.orfeo-schmuck.de/aktuelles.html
Ornamentum (New York)	http://www.ornamentumgallery.com
Pieces Of Eight (Melbourne)	http://www.piecesofeight.com.au
Plateaux (London)	http://www.plateaux.co.uk
Platina (Stockholm)	http://www.platina.se
Plumiage (Groningen)	http://www.pluimage.nl
Pontenplas (Ghent)	http://www.pontenplas.be
Prime (Toronto)	http://www.primegallery.ca
Ra (Amsterdam)	http://www.galerie-ra.nl
Rantapaja (Lappeenranta)	http://corrie.scp.fi/koru1/rantapaja.htm
Reverso (Lisbon)	http://www.reversodasbernardas.com
Sculpture To Wear (Santa Monica)	http://www.sculpturetowear.com
Shaw (Northeast Harbor, Maine)	http://www.shawjewelry.com
Shibuichi (Palmeira)	http://www.shibuichi.com
Sintra (Gothenburg)	http://www.sintra.o.se
So (Solothurn)	http://www.galerieso.com
Spandau (Berlin)	http://www.galerie-spandow.de
Spektrum (Munich)	http://www.galerie-spektrum.de
Tactus (Copenhagen)	http://www.galerietactus.com
Treykorn (Berlin)	http://www.treykorn.de
Verzameldwerk (Ghent)	http://www.verzameldwerk.be
Villa De Bondt (Ghent)	http://www.villadebondt.be
Uzupio (Vilnius)	http://www.uzupiogalerija.lt
Velvet da Vinci (San Francisco)	http://www.velvetdavinci.com
Vice Versa (Lausanne)	http://www.viceversa.ch
Wittenbrink (Munich)	http://www.galeriewittenbrink.de

Glossary

Abrasive heads points made of emery or carborundum, shafted so that they can be fitted into a power tool and used for carving

Alabaster a soft stone similar in appearance to marble

Amber not a stone at all, but fossilised tree resin from extinct coniferous trees

Amulet a worn object attributed with magical value

Annealing the process of heating metal to a point where it relieves the strains created when working the metal, making it more malleable.

Araldite a brand of epoxy resin adhesive

Argillite a fine-grained sedimentary rock composed predominantly of clay

Bezel a form of setting where an object is surrounded by a thin metal wall

Binding wire iron wire used to secure a piece of metal for soldering

Bivalve a class of mollusc

Black amber a kind of jet

Bog wood partly fossilised wood extracted from tree trunks that have been buried in peat bogs and preserved from decay by the acidic and anaerobic bog conditions

Bony amber a cloudy amber

Burnisher handheld steel tool used to polish, push and harden metal

Cameo a carving in shell of contrasting colour layers

Carborundum manmade abrasive stone

Carded fleece that has been prepared for felting by combing with a carder

Casting pouring molten metal into a mould so that it cools in the shape of the mould

Centrifugal machine a casting machine that spins, forcing molten metal into the mould

Charcoal block a soldering block that can also be used for casting

Claw setting an open setting using wire

Collet *see* **Bezel**

Cold connections methods of joining without solder or torch work

Copal semi-fossilised resin amber obtained from various tropical trees

Coral the hornlike skeleton of marine animals called polyps

Cuttlefish the backplate of a squid, used in cuttlefish casting

Dopstick a short stick to one end of which an object is cemented while being worked on

Ear plug in jewellery, an ornament secured through a perforation in the earlobe

Glossary

Electroforming the electrical process of coating an object in a thin layer of metal

Electroplating the electrical process of coating an object in a thick layer of metal

Embossed a raised pattern

Emery paper an abrasive paper used to clean, polish and texture surfaces

Epoxy a strong slow- or quick-drying adhesive resin

Ferrotype a photographic process developed in the 19th century, also called the tintype or melainotype

Flexible drive shaft movable cable transmitting electrical power to a cutting tool

Flush level with the surrounding surface

Gastropod a species of mollusc including most animals that produce shells

Grit rough particles of varying grades on abrasive papers

Greywacke a variety of sandstone characterised by its hardness, dark colour and poorly sorted, angular grains of quartz

Gutta-percha a natural latex produced from the sap of the gutta-percha tree

Hardwood wood from broad-leaved trees

Heartwood the inert or dead portion of a living tree

Inclusion a trapped object

Inlay to fit one material into the face of another

Iridescence the quality of reflecting light in various hues

Jade a green hardstone also known as 'New Zealand greenstone'

Jet a geological material formed from decaying wood under extreme pressure, also referred to as 'black amber'

Knot an imperfection in wood stemming from the growth of a branch

Labret an object worn in a perforation in the lip

Lathe a machine for shaping wood or metal

Linseed oil used to polish and soften materials

Lubricant a substance that reduces friction, e.g. oil or water

Lustre the way light interacts with the surface of a mineral or gemstone

Malleable a characteristic of materials that allows them to be formed and shaped without breaking or splitting

Marble a metamorphic rock often used for carving

Metamorphic rock rock formed deep beneath the Earth's surface under great stress from high pressures and temperatures

Mohs scale a scale of hardness ranging from 1 to 10

Mother-of-pearl *see Nacre*

Nacre a naturally occurring composite of calcium carbonate produced by shells, also known as mother-of-pearl

Neatsfoot oil yellow oil rendered from the feet and shin bones of cattle, used as a conditioner, softener and preservative for leather

New Zealand greenstone *see Pounamu*

Oxidised A type of patina on the surface of a metal giving it a dark metallic look

Particulate respirator mouth-and-nose mask providing protection from harmful airborne particles through the filtration of tiny particles

Parchment thin calf-, sheep- or goatskin that is not tanned

Pickle weak sulphuric acid used to remove flux and oxides from annealed or soldered metal

Pinchbeck an alloy made of copper and zinc

Polishing to bring up to a high shine

Pounamu (New Zealand greenstone) highly prized hard nephrite jade, mid-to-dark green in colour, found in New Zealand and parts of Australia.

Prong setting similar to a claw setting, but using prongs

Pyrography the technique of using a heated tip or wire to burn or scorch designs onto natural materials such as wood or leather

Rapid prototyping the automatic construction of physical objects using solid freeform fabrication and computer-aided design

Rawhide animal skin exposed to the tanning process

Riveting a joining method that does not involve soldering

Rivets the elements used to join pieces when riveting

Roll-printing creating patterns and textures on the metal surface by exerting even pressure using a rolling mill

Rouge finely powdered copper oxide used for polishing

Sapwood living wood in a growing tree

Saw-piercing cutting metal using a jeweller's saw

Score to mark a line using a sharp-ended steel tool

Serrated a grooved cutting edge

Setting surrounding an object with sheet metal or prongs in order to protect and secure it

Soapstone a soft stone composed of talc, also known as 'steatite'

Softwood wood from conifer trees

Splaying to prise open and apart

Steatite *see Soapstone*

Talisman a protective jewel to which magical properties are attributed

Tanning the chemical process of preserving skin, preventing decomposition and often imparting colour, it is part of the leather production process

Tiki a carved talisman of humanoid form, common to the Polynesian cultures of the Pacific Ocean

Vellum calfskin that has not been tanned (imitation vellum is made of cotton)

Suppliers

Fleece

Scottish Fibres
23 Damhead Lothianburn
Edinburgh EH10 7EA
www.scottishfibres.co.uk

Wingham Wool Work
70 Main Street
Wentworth
Yorkshire S62 7TN
www.winghamwoolwork.co.uk

Tools & equipment

Walsh Brothers
118–120 High Street
Beckenham,
Kent BR3 1EB
www.walshbrothers.co.uk

Sutton Tools
37 Frederick Street
Birmingham B1 3HN
www.suttontools.co.uk

Tools, precious metals, findings

Argex Ltd
130 Hockley Hill
Birmingham B18 5AN
www.argex.co.uk

Blundells & Sons
199 Wardour Street
London W1V 4JN
www.jblundell.co.uk

Cooksons Precious Metals
49 Hatton Garden
London EC1N 8YS
www.cooksongold.com

Rashbel
24–28 Hatton Wall,
London EC1N 8JN
www.rashbel.com

Wood & shell inlay supplies

Original Marquetry
143 Bishopthorpe Road,
Westbury-On-Trym,
Bristol
BS10 5AF
www.originalmarquetry.co.uk

USA

Metalliferous
34 West 46th Street
New York, NY 10036
Telephone: +1 (212) 944 0909
Website: www.metalliferous.com

Belgium

Swiss Axe
Rijfstraat 11
B2018 Antwerpen
Telephone: +32 (0)3 232 10 90
Website: www.swissaxe.be
Email: info@swissaxe.be

The Netherlands

Bijou Moderne
Edisonlaan 36-38
2665 JC Bleiswijk
Telephone: +31 (0)10-5296600
Email: info@bijoumoderne.nl
Website: www.bijoumoderne.nl

Germany

Karl Fischer GmbH
Berliner Strasse 18
Postfach 567
D-75105 Pforzheim
Telephone: +49 (0)72 31 31 0 31
Email: info@fischer-pforzheim.de
Website: www.fischer-pforzheim.de

Selected Bibliography

Anderson, Patricia, *Contemporary Jewellery in Australia and New Zealand*, Craftsman House, 1998

Chalker, Kari, *Totems to turquoise: Native North American jewellery arts of the Northwest and Southwest*, American Museum of Natural History, 2004

Dormer, Peter, *The New Jewellery*, Thames & Hudson,

English, Helen & Dormer, Peter, *Jewellery of Our Time*, Thames & Hudson, 1995

Fraquent, Helen, *Amber*, Butterworths, 1987

Gale, Emma & Little, Ann, *Jewellery Making*, Hodder & Stoughton, 2000

Hamby, Louise, *Art on a String: Threaded Objects from the Central Desert and Arnhem*, Australian Centre for Craft & Design, 2001

Jargstorf, Sibylle, *Ethnic Jewellery from Africa, Europe & Asia*, Schiffer, 2000

Joris, Yvonne, *Jewels of Mind & Mentality*, Rotterdam Museum, 2000

Junger, Herman, *Found Treasures*, Thames & Hudson, 2003

Keene, Manuel, *Treasury of the World*, Thames & Hudson, 2001

Mack, John, *Ethnic Jewellery*, British Museum publication,1988

Ogden, Jack, *Jewellery of the Ancient World*, Trefoil, 1982

Index

aboriginal 16
Africa 13-14
alabaster 30-32
Alleweireldt, An 55, 99-100
Amazonian 14, 17-18
amber 13, 57-60, 77, 116-117
Americas, the 16
amulet 7, 12, 18-19, 124
anti-gold ethos 21
araldite 90-1
Arcy-Sur-Cure 10
argillite 16, 19

Bak, Kirsten 52, 101
Barteldres, Maike 96
basalt 16
Bauer, Ela 3, 39, 60, 102-3
Beeler, Kristin 47
Bezant, Laura 63
bezel-setting 59, 77-80
bivalve 39
black amber 20, 56-7
Blombos Cave 9-10, 12
Blu-Tack 27, 78
bone 14-15, 17-19, 37, 42-7
bony amber 57
Buescher, Sebastian 38, 41, 62, 104-5
burnisher 78, 80

carving 30-4, 47, 52-4, 59, 119
casting 89, 91, 94-6
centrifugal machine 96
charcoal block 85-7, 94-5

chisel 52, 88
clamp 79, 88
claw setting 81
cold connections 59, 73-93
copal 57
coral 19, 39-41, 127-8
cuttlefish 94

drill bit 36, 44

ebony 14, 134
Eichenberg, Iris 42, 66, 107-8
electroforming 96-7
electroplating 96-7
embossed 97
emery paper 45, 78, 80, 83-4
epoxy 39, 85-7, 90-2

feather 17-18, 57, 70-72, 115-6
felting 66-70
flush 80, 82, 89
fur 17

gastropod 39
Girvan, Grace 80
greywacke 16
grit 34, 45, 60
grizzly bear 18
gutta-percha 20

Hackney, Katy 109
hair 19-20, 25, 57, 64, 111
hair sticks 18

hardwood 42, 49, 98
heartwood 50
hei tiki 50
hide 61
Holt, Caroline 45, 56
horn 42-7
Houtu, Piritta 110
Huan, Hsiu Hsuan 22, 111
huia feather 15

Iannuzzi, Ornella 106-7
inlay 82-6, 89
inuit 18-19
ivory 14, 16, 18-19, 42-3, 55

jade 15-16, 30-31, 126
Jensen, Mette 112
jet 20, 55-7, 134

King, Sarah 82, 87
knot 51

labret 14, 19
latex 20, 60
lathe 60
leather 25, 63-4, 98
ledge-setting 80
Legg, Beth 8, 25, 36, 44, 72, 89, 95, 113
Lewis, Anna 71-2, 115-6

Macleod, Alison 92
Maori 15-16
marble 19, 30
Marden, Hayley 93

Masai 13
McCallum, Kelly 46
metamorphic rock 30, 32
Mohs scale 39, 57
Mogensen, Helga Ragnhildur 49
Mollenuir, Julie 40, 56, 58, 116
mother-of-pearl 22, 82-3, 87
mourning jewellery 19-20

nacre 37, 39
neanderthal 10
neatsfoot oil 64
nephrite 16, 18
New Zealand greenstone 16
Nijland, Evert 56, 118, 119

ochre 9, 16

Pacific 14
Papua New Guinea 15
parchment 62
particulate respirator 28
pickle 97
pinchbeck 20
Pinchuk, Natalya 119-20
polishing 16, 28, 34, 41, 43, 45, 82
Polynesian 15
Pond, Jo 61
prong setting 81
pyrography 98

quartz 121
quartzite 19

Rannik, Kaire 54
rawhide 61
riveting 47, 73-6
rivets 59, 73-6

roll-printing 97

Saarnia, Laura 35, 121
sapwood 50
Sarneel, Lucy 24, 38, 77, 122-3
Schreiber, Constanze 65, 124-5
seeds 13, 16-18
serpentine 19
setting 77-81, 87
Sheehan, Joe 33, 35, 74, 126-7
shell 9-12, 14-18, 28, 37-8, 40-41, 77, 82-6, 94, 127
soapstone 19, 30, 32
softwood 49
Speckner, Bettina 23, 37, 41, 127-8
splaying 73, 75
steatite 30
stone 16-18, 25, 28, 30-6, 82, 110, 130-1
string 14, 16, 59, 85

talisman 7, 11-12, 19
tanning 98
Tiitsar, Ketli 76
Tolvanen, Terhi 21, 48, 53, 59, 79, 128-30
tortoiseshell 19
turquoise 16, 82
Tuupanen, Tarja 6, 31, 34, 130-1

Van der Donk, Jacomyn 131-32
vellum 62
Victorian 19, 55

Willemstijn, Francis 20, 49,

73, 133-4
wood 14-16, 18-19, 22, 25, 28, 48-55, 57, 77, 82, 98, 112
wool 64-6, 108, 119-20

Yokouchi, Sayumi 134-5